Effective
Learning
in Schools
. . .

How to Integrate Learning
and Leadership for a
Successful School

CHRISTOPHER BOWRING-CARR
AND JOHN WEST-BURNHAM

An imprint of **Pearson Education**
London · New York · San Francisco · Toronto · Sydney
Tokyo · Singapore · Hong Kong · Cape Town · Madrid
Paris · Milan · Munich · Amsterdam

For Frances, as ever
To Phyllis West-Burnham, with love

Edge Hill College Library X

Author

Class No.

Book No. 667185

PEARSON EDUCATION LIMITED

Edinburgh Gate
Harlow CM20 2JE
Tel: +44 (0)1279 623623
Fax: +44 (0)1279 431059
Website: www.pearsoned.co.uk

First published in Great Britain in 1997

© Pearson Education Limited 1997

The right of Christopher Bowring-Carr and John West-Burnham
to be identified as Authors of this Work has been asserted by them
in accordance with the Copyright, Designs and Patents Act 1988.

ISBN 0 273 62413 X

British Library Cataloguing in Publication Data
A CIP catalogue record for this book can be obtained from the British Library

All rights reserved; no part of this publication may be reproduced, stored
in a retrieval system, or transmitted in any form or by any means, electronic,
mechanical, photocopying, recording, or otherwise without either the prior
written permission of the Publishers or a licence permitting restricted copying
in the United Kingdom issued by the Copyright Licensing Agency Ltd,
90 Tottenham Court Road, London W1T 4LP. This book may not be lent,
resold, hired out or otherwise disposed of by way of trade in any form
of binding or cover other than that in which it is published, without the
prior consent of the Publishers.

10 9

Typeset by Phoenix Photosetting, Chatham, Kent
Printed and bound in Great Britain by Bookcraft (Bath) Ltd, Midsomer Norton, Somerset

The Publishers' policy is to use paper manufactured from sustainable forests.

Contents

■ ■ ■

Preface *vii*

1 Tomorrow's School *1*

2 An Overview *22*

3 Our Children's World *37*

4 Understanding Learning *60*

5 Learning: The Variables *87*

6 Leadership for Learning *116*

7 In-service Development *138*

8 Transforming Schools *152*

References *164*

Index *167*

Preface

■ ■ ■

Throughout this book, we challenge many of the prevailing orthodoxies in the world of education. We will be attempting to change the meanings and the emotional surrounds of many of the words that are at the core of the language of education. What follows are the main principles upon which this book is based. There is a danger in giving a list; it is easy to assume that it implies an ascending or descending order of importance. With this list there is no such order; the items are inter-connected, each item reflecting one or more aspects of other items and in turn being reflected in them.

First, knowledge grows out of the curiosity and involvement of the individual, and out of the educative relationship of teacher and learner; it cannot be mandated from a centralised hierarchy, and it cannot be pinned like some dead specimen. It follows, therefore, that acquired knowledge – knowledge that has been sought for and created by the learner – is more significant, valid and long-lasting than received knowledge.

Second, in the context of a rapidly changing world, in a world in which information and knowledge expand, shift and create new boundaries and territories with such bewildering speed, 'learning how to learn' is *the* most important outcome of education. Closely linked to this principle is a cluster of four others. First, learning is, at the same time, both an individual, subjective and contingent process, and a communal process. Second, the existing mind-map of the learner is the starting point for all true education. Third, teaching is one of the factors which influence learning, but it is not the prime determinant. Fourth, only a small proportion of learning can take place in schools.

We stress in many places in the book the rapidly increasing volume of information; however, as information increases, its half-life diminishes, and so the need to interrogate and manage information becomes proportionately more important; memorisation is best left to computers.

The quality of leadership in the school or college is paramount. Leadership is to learning what management is to the curriculum. Finally, in that learning community, all are learners, and all learners are equal.

Christopher Bowring-Carr and John West-Burnham

1

■ ■ ■

Tomorrow's School

Let the main object of this, our Didactic, be as follows: To seek and to find a method of instruction, by which teachers may teach less, but learners learn more; by which schools may be the scene of less noise, aversion, and useless labour, but of more leisure, enjoyment, and solid progress . . . (John Amos Comenius, 'The Great Didactic', in Charles E. Silberman, *Crisis in the Classroom*)

What follows in this chapter is pure fiction, but it is fiction based on what some schools are doing at present, on the theories of learning put forward in this book, and on extrapolation from trends visible in the present. All the technology that is mentioned in this chapter is available now, though not necessarily in the educational format implied here. However, it is not the technology that is important; it merely enables a particular approach to the management of learning to be put in place. The school that is described is a place in which learning is at the centre of the organisation; it is not a school coming out of science fiction, but one which is not too far from what some schools are striving towards today. The dictum 'form follows function' is taken to a logical conclusion. Certain rules and regulations have been assumed to have melted away, or been destroyed, and people are shown to be happy in an organisation that is far looser and less rule-bound than any we are accustomed to in the world of education at the moment. It is a 'loose-tight' organisation – 'loose' in its day-to-day rules, and flexible even about those that are in place; 'tight' in the adherence to a strong vision, one of learning being at the centre, and of everyone and everything being framed by that drive. This is, however, a version of the flexible learning organisation that is needed if we are going to enable our young people not only to learn what they need for their lives in the twenty-first century but also, and perhaps more importantly, enable our young people to learn in ways that they need to imbibe from their earliest years so that they are emotionally and intellectually equipped to cope with the demands that their lives will make of them. They also need to see how learning can be fun and form an essential and continuous part of their lives. Of course, far more is packed into this single day-in-the-life-of Midtown College than would in fact occur; it is a compressed sample.

Midtown College

Midtown is a pleasant market town in the north of England, not far from the Scottish borders. It is the meeting-place for the people from the small towns and villages scattered on the fells and in the valleys around. Despite being only thirty or so miles from Newcastle, it has maintained a strong identity, and boasts a range of amenities and clubs and societies. One of the institutions in which the inhabitants had a very considerable pride was the comprehensive school. It was a genuine comprehensive with all but a very small handful of the children of the area going there. The locals' pride arose in part from the excellent examination results, comparable to any grammar school in those parts of the country still retaining the selective system, and in part from the fact that it was a thoroughly pleasant, cheerful place to be in. The children and the adults clearly were happy to be there, and the headteacher maintained an easy, relaxed pace which belied the very hard work that was expected and achieved. It was a thoroughly good school.

Some time ago, it changed its title to the Midtown Community College, as it widened its range of courses, and ran a three-session day. Students in the sixth form were able to choose to which two of the three sessions they wanted to go , and their choice depended upon the mix of courses that they opted for. Adults became an increasingly usual sight in GCSE classes and 'A' level classes, as well as non-examination groups, and the term 'student' was easily used for anyone taking a course, examination-bound or not, in the college. The school string quartet played regularly in the town church, which doubled as the local concert hall, and the town band, in which there were students and people from the town, could be relied upon to help out at functions which took place in the school grounds. Slowly but steadily, most of the barriers that had, in previous times, so often come between a school and its community had been eroded, without anyone really being aware of the changes or of feeling the need to fight any battles to defend the old walls. As the barriers vanished, and the range of activities on the campus widened, the name changed again. It became the Midtown Community Centre, and emotionally and intellectually it was ready for the enormous changes that were to come about just after the new millennium had been welcomed.

It was 7:15 in the morning, and Midtown Community Centre was coming to life. Judith walked through the office-cum-lodge into the quadrangle that was formed by the old Victorian building facing her, and the two blocks of newer buildings that were on either side. She was going to the crèche, two rooms on the bottom floor of the left-hand building, where she would help for the first part of the day. In part, she did the work as it paid her some pocket money, and in part she did it because she was finding it increasingly an interesting and rewarding job. It also contributed to a section of her study package, and towards the end of next month she expected to be ready to take the first stage of the child-care examination. As she passed through the gatehouse she pressed her palm on one of the register-screens and logged on to the computer for the day.

She reached the small office to the side of the crèche, chatted briefly to the other two who were cleaning up and getting toys and games ready, and then plugged in her lap-top to see if there were any messages. Everywhere you went in the school, there were points at which you could plug in your lap-top. The two main alterations to the buildings had been the enormous quantity of wiring that had been installed, and the creation, out of all those near-identical, box-shaped rooms, of as many rooms of different sizes as the architect could manage. 'Flexible learning – flexible rooms' was one of the slogans of the first headteacher of Midtown after the Education Act of 2003.

Judith had three messages waiting for her. The first was from her learning manager asking her to come to her office at 12:15 for their weekly talk. There were group tutorial sessions for everyone each morning, and a one-to-one session with a tutor/learning manager (the terms were used interchangeably) once a week. The second message was from her seven-year-old buddy whom she listened to reading every week, saying that three o'clock was fine, and could she please come to room 18. The third was a stiff note from the French teacher saying that her paper was now three days late and there would be fireworks if she did not e-mail it to him that day. Judith entered the two appointments into her lap-top so that it would remind her, and hurriedly called up the French paper that she had only just completed late the previous evening. She e-mailed it to the teacher and added an apologetic note.

For the next hour she worked steadily with her friends, cleaning and tidying, and then welcoming the first customers of the day. At around 8:30 she went to the canteen to get her breakfast and see a couple of her friends whom she always met there. At about the same time, Simon, who taught some English, was making his way to the drama studio where he was hoping to be allowed to help with an up-coming video of local music and stories. The group was made up of two students from the centre, a well-known player of the Northumbrian pipes, and the 17-year-old who had proved herself a first-rate producer of musical shows which concentrated on local and border music. The team hoped that if they could make it interesting enough, and if the quality was up to standard, they would be able to get it onto the local school cable network, and, possibly, if it was really good, onto the Northern Schools' Network, but that was being very optimistic. As he got in, they were looking at a video they had recorded the previous evening from a school in Cumbria which had done a programme on some geological features of the western end of Hadrian's wall. The standard was superb, and depressed them.

'OK, so that's the technical target we've got to meet,' one of the group was saying gloomily. 'We're really rather good on the musical side of things, but we're just amateurs on the technical side. Let's call up that Carlisle school and have a conf with them and pick their brains.'

They agreed and Toni, the producer, went off to arrange a time when they could use one of the video-conference rooms. The video-conferencing centre had been the brainchild of the present headteacher, Ruth. At the time she had first suggested the idea, there had been considerable controversy. People could understand that there might be the need for one room, but to put up a new building with seven such rooms seemed a wild extravagance. However, Ruth had stuck with the idea, raised the money from a number of sources, and equipped it lavishly with the very latest technology. The gamble paid off handsomely. From the first, business people from all over the North-East and North-West and from the Borders had seen the benefits of leasing one or more of the rooms. The centre's budget had benefited considerably from these leases. However, it was with the arrival of a new university that the centre became the focus of very considerable activity and became a major source of finance. Following examples in the United States, Canada and the Nordic countries, it was decided to establish the Northern University of the Air. The university was to have no campus, just a collection of offices in Carlisle and Newcastle; all its lectures, seminars and tutorials were to be handled through teleconferencing and wide area networks, and, of course, it had its site on the Internet. One of the main teleconferencing centres became Midtown Community Centre, conveniently placed as it was for students from a wide geographical area. The centre benefited not only financially, but also because its students could access university-level work when they were ready, and complete some modules towards a first degree while still nominally in the centre.

Another of the great advantages that the centre students had over their equivalents in the mid-twentieth century was the range of contacts they had available. There was a local area network for the town and surroundings; there was a second, which covered the north of England, and then, through the Internet, there was the worldwide system. Once the simple-minded idea that 'market forces' and the concomitant competition was the best way to improve education had been dumped, schools very rapidly saw how cooperation gave each student an enormously increased range of possibilities. Anyone with a particular interest could, through the networks, share enthusiasms, learn with someone from a different country, see things from totally new angles; the range of information was unlimited, and students could have horizons as wide as their imagination and that of their tutors and coaches could stretch.

The headteacher was having breakfast in the canteen with a group of three or four people involved in the local tourist business and two students who were going to do a study for them that summer into where tourists were coming from. They were discussing ways in which they could capture the data, the object being to find out if they could target their advertising more specifically.

The students could use the experience they gained towards a module in their statistics course.

'OK', said the head. 'I think that's pretty clear. You'll obviously need some flexi time.' She turned to the two students. 'How long do you think you'll need to set up the program?'

'We talked this over yesterday evening, and we reckon a week should see us ready. Does that seem reasonable?'

'Yes, that's fine. Let your learning managers know as soon as you can. Good luck.' She turned to the business people. 'Once you've got your data and you know what sort of a campaign you want to mount, you'll remember that the local community newspaper is published here, won't you? Our technology is really pretty good. If you want good quality flyers or leaflets or brochures, or anything like that, we can do them for you, and at a rather better price than you'll get elsewhere. We've got first-rate video equipment too, and we can put you on the Internet.'

The business people smiled, and one of them said, 'You should have gone into business. You really know how to sell.'

'There's nothing wrong with being businesslike about education, as long as means and ends are never confused.'

She got up, shook hands with them all, and started to leave the cafeteria. Every few steps, though, she stopped to chat, ask a question, congratulate; it was a slow progress. It was like this every day and for as much of the day as she could possibly manage. Mostly she was out and about, as that was the only way she could feel that she was in touch, and could let everyone know that she was interested and involved.

By now the campus was beginning to get crowded. All the students under 18 were expected to start the day at nine o'clock by going to their tutor room where they spent the first 20 minutes of the day. Tutor groups were kept to a maximum of 15, to ensure that the tutor, or learning manager, would have every chance of getting to know the group well, and therefore be able to identify each student's learning styles, strengths and areas of difficulty, and thereby chart the individual's course. Such a ratio was achieved by using every teacher available, including the head and the deputy. Some time ago this system of tutoring had been identified as the essential core of the individualised approach to the curriculum, and so every resource had been directed into it. The administrative trivia that in times past had cluttered up tutor time had been removed; the 20 minutes were dedicated to one-to-one, small group, and occasionally whole-group, talk, focused on the students' learning.

Robert met his tutor group in an office that for the rest of the day was used by the community newspaper team; it was not perhaps the best possible location as it was usually untidy, but every location was pressed into service for tutor-group time. The group was made up of students of different ages, the youngest being 11 and the oldest 18. At one time, there had been a discussion about the possibility of including adults in the tutor groups as they were to be found in most of the groups for every other activity. However, in the end it was felt that the range of difficulties would be too wide, and the potential for embarrassment too great. Adults had their own tutor groups which met in the early evening. Robert plugged in his lap-top and opened up his tutor file.

'Good morning, all. Can you give me a couple of minutes, as I want to talk to John, and then we can have a general chat and see how things are going. John, I wonder if I could have a moment with you.'

John went over to the table where Robert was sitting.

'I'm sorry to have to start the day off like this, but there have been two or three complaints from Wendy about you. You seem to delight in baiting her, and getting her angry. Can you tell me anything about it?'

John looked faintly embarrassed.

'It's just too easy, I suppose. I find that I can get through the work really easily, and then, before I get on with another part of it, I get out of the program and look around for some fun. She's the easy target. Oh, I guess she's super with the ones that find it difficult, but for the few of us that steam ahead, she doesn't seem to know how to cope. Sorry.'

'Can't go on like that, you know. As you say you find the work all that easy, I think I'd better talk to your maths coach and we'll sort out another track for you. You're good at maths, and I don't want to see you wasting your time, and I certainly don't want to see you making life difficult for Wendy and the rest of the group. In the meantime, you will find Wendy today, and you will apologise, and you will not bait her again. Understood?'

John agreed and joined the remainder of the group.

'Right, let's see how things are going. Marianne, I've got a note here to ask you about your American project. How's it going?'

'Really well. I made contact with a boy in one of the schools that we're twinned with, and he's just as interested as I am, and we've swapped a lot of material.'

'Which school is that?'

'The high school in Virginia. I've decided that I'm going to concentrate on the Union Army's string of failures at the start of the Civil War, try to analyse what went wrong and then what happened to get things turned round. I've got masses of material, and then Josh – he's the American boy – sent me some marvellous stuff from the Smithsonian, but I just need time to sort it and order it. Can I have time-out?'

'How long will you want?'

'Two weeks should see me through,' Marianne said.

'Let me see.' He opened the file on Marianne, and saw that she had 'time-out' three months ago to finalise a module in science. She had completed the module, and done very well in the examination that she chose to do straight afterwards, and then had successfully caught up with her other work. 'That looks good, Marianne. At the end of this session, would you go and make contact with your coach and see if he can help at all. And when you've nearly finished, do let me have a look. I did American history as a subsidiary at university and I'd love to see what conclusions you come to. You'll have the benefit of a far wider range of material than was available to me.'

For some time, the school had had a system of coaches. It was perfectly clear that the full-time teachers in the school could not possibly cope with all the interests and different avenues that the students were following, so the headteacher and a range of contacts all over the world had set up a system of coaches. A database had been established, which was constantly growing, listing people with a particular expertise in one area or another. When a student expressed the desire to follow a subject in the depth of detail with which no one in the centre could help, then the database was consulted and the student put in touch with the coach. The power of enthusiast working with enthusiast was very considerable, and many deep friendships had grown from a shared passion for a subject.

'I'd love to. Josh and I are going to have a talk and browse through some of the material this evening – he seems to go to bed at all sorts of odd hours – and that should help to get me started. Did I tell you? My coach is really great. He's a retired Admiral in the US Navy, who is a Civil War buff. Boy – he seems to know the first name of pretty well everyone who fought that war. Well, OK, so I exaggerate, but he's really great. He's just so patient, and well, he's sort of like a big bear.'

The group laughed. Marianne always thought her coaches, male and female, were like big bears.

'That's fine, Marianne. Amit, how about you? Things going well?'

'Yes, fine, thanks. Yesterday, Hamish and I started the new module in the design course, and we were working in the CAD centre, but then our coach suggested that we transfer to the more sophisticated stuff in his lab in Prague. You should have seen it. I mean – linking memories by plasma loops. Amazing!'

Robert laughed. 'I haven't a clue what you're talking about, Amit, but all the reports that I'm getting say that you're doing really well. I suppose you'll be asking your parents for the fare to Prague next.'

'Oh, yes. I'd love to go. And when I was talking to my parents yesterday about what we've been doing, they both said that they'll come too. They're mad about Baroque music. Yes, I want to go because I'd really like to meet our coach and visit his lab.'

'I think I'll join you. Never been. So – Haresh – how go things?'

'Not bad. I think that spell on the farm last month gave me the background on fertilisers that I needed. It all seemed pretty remote on screen.'

'You've lost me, Haresh,' said Robert. 'What fertiliser?'

'Don't you remember? I asked the Accreditation Centre to set up an exam for me for the end of June, and then I got terribly stuck on really understanding the downside of certain fertilisers in run-off situations. I mean the theory was clear enough, and the graphics and simulations were fine, but I asked to go and spend some time really seeing it first-hand, and my coach knew this farmer in South Wales, and I spent some time with him.'

'Yes, fine. I remember now. Well, is the accred still on?'

'Yes. I'm taking it tomorrow and the mix is really good. Two theory bits and then a viva with a chap in some lab in South East Australia. I feel pretty good.'

In the past, examinations were held at the same time for all the students when they reached a particular age. This bizarre arrangement meant that when a student was 16, for example, regardless of whether they were ready or not, they took examinations in all the subjects that they were studying at the time. In other walks of life, music, car driving, sports for example, people took examinations when they were ready. Furthermore, in the old days the examinations were the same for all pupils, and focused on the students' responses to unseen questions rather than allowing them to demonstrate their mastery of a topic. Last, and by no means least, the examinations did not prove that a student could actually *do* anything with the material being tested. This system had, of course, been abandoned. Now, students, with their learning managers and subject teachers and, when appropriate, with their coaches, decide when they are ready to undertake 'learning accreditation', as it is called. They would then get into contact with an Accreditation Centre, as the old examination boards were now labelled, and one of the specialists would, with the student's learning manager, decide how the student would demonstrate mastery. Furthermore, the test embraced a variety of methods. The method might be a straight paper on a historical topic, but the paper could be expanded by a student-created CD disc showing, say, a series of maps charting the course of an important battle. The student's work could then be taken up by the tester who might have a viva voce with the student to probe the depth of their understanding of the subject matter, and explore how far the student had delved into the surrounds of the topic to add to that understanding. In other subject areas, the student might submit a video of an experiment that they had undertaken, with the student's voice-over describing and justifying the methodology. In another area, the year's work in the form of a portfolio of artwork could be presented on CD, with the student's own background music. In short, the idea was to enable the student to demonstrate mastery of a topic in ways which helped the student to show his or her best work, and in ways that did not favour a written response over all others.

Another outcome was that the old idea that a 'broad and balanced' curriculum resulted from having a collection of nine or ten subject labels on the timetable was scrapped. It had long been realised that in most of the subjects the same learning and teaching strategies had been employed, and the same two intelligences predominated – the verbal and the logico-scientific. Now students could take one topic, investigate it in depth, and by doing so explore three or four areas of experience, and stretch and employ a range of intelligences.

At first, there had been furious reaction against such an accreditation scheme. It was felt that only by the 'tried-and-tested' examination system could standards be maintained. There were many who said that the 'gold standard' was being abandoned. However, when it was seen that the new approach was, in fact, far more rigorous, the opposition slowly subsided. No longer could an examination be passed by intensive cramming for three weeks before the day; no longer could a class 'mug up' on expected questions. No longer could a teacher's notes, unaltered for years, be used as the basis of a year's work in the sure and certain knowledge that the end-of-year examination would most certainly be yet another variation on a well-known theme.

'That's great, Haresh. Hope it goes well. Before we break up, one bit of good news, and one not so good. The good news is that the work Darryl and Sue did on producing a short video about bird nests for the first-year kids in St John's went down really well, and has gone into their resource bank. And that work is going to count towards their English and arts modules, too. Well done. The not-so-good news is about your late work, Derek. It's happened too often. I've arranged to go round to your home this evening, and your mother and father and you and I are going to thrash this business out once and for all. See you at 5:00. Right, it's 9:20. You'd better move on to whatever is next for you. Thank you, and enjoy your day.'

Fifteen lap-tops snapped open as they all checked to see what they had planned for the remainder of the day. Robert's was already open, and he checked his day.

His main subject was history, but he had become very interested in learning Spanish in order to do some original research, and was also trying hard to lose some weight and get a little fitter. His day was as follows:

09:40–10:40	History Group 3. (This was a group of ten students, studying the Industrial Revolution. They met three times a week, mostly for seminar-type work, papers having been e-mailed to him ahead of the meeting.)
10:40–11:30	Meet with his fitness coach in the gym and have a session.
11:30–11:45	Break.
11:45–12:15	One-to-one session with his Spanish tutor, one of the school's modern language team.
12:20–13:00	History Group 5.
13:00–14:00	Lunch.
14:00–15:00	Tutor team meeting. Each tutor team was made up of seven tutors chosen so as to ensure coverage of every curricular area of experience.

15:00–17:00	Free, but this time was used when necessary for home visiting, or seeing some of his tutor group who were doing placement work in the area. It was also time to catch up with e-mail, responding to student papers and tracking down material for the research he was doing into the Spanish conquest of Mexico.
17:00–18:00	Evening meal.
18:00–18:30 18:30–19:00 19:30–20:00	Three short sessions with various history groups to check and discuss progress.

His days varied – sometimes ending in the early afternoon, sometimes not until 9:30 in the evening. Overall he supposed that he was working rather longer hours than his counterparts did 20 or 30 years ago, but the longer hours were in part taken up with his own studies and with recreational activity, such as his fitness class, that were allowed to count towards his total contract hours. Of course, there were no hours laid down by government; everyone was on an individual short-term contract. He was on his second three-year contract, and was hoping that the next would be a five-year one. That was the maximum for anyone, including the head. He liked it in Midtown, and wanted to stay on.

Judith finished her breakfast and went to her tutorial. She wanted to talk to her tutor about finding a coach for a special project she was wanting to start. Her studies were centred on drama – by the age of 18 she had built up a good spread of results over the last four years, and was now concentrating for a year on her special love. Apart from acting and beginning her training in stage management, she was studying the theatre in the Restoration period, and was hoping to find a coach who knew the subject well and could help guide her reading and suggest a starting point in studying the plays that she could access through her cable TV at home.

Appropriately enough, her tutorial was in the small drama studio that was jointly used by the school and the town's drama society. It was in the town about ten minutes from the school, and she walked there with three of her tutor group. On arrival, Judith talked to Ellen, her tutor, about her need for a coach, and Ellen promised to start a search by e-mailing a lecturer in the English faculty at Newcastle University whom she knew. He might be able to find someone who was willing to become a coach. As more and more schools in the world took up the idea of extending the curriculum, it was becoming a little more difficult to find coaches willing and able to meet the demands of the students. Ellen said that she might be able to have an answer by the time the one-to-one tutorial came up later that day.

After the tutorial, Judith went home to settle down to complete writing a paper (the old term stuck tenaciously). She had to get it to her drama teacher in time for him to read it and then they and the other four in the group would discuss it at the next session. The deadline was that afternoon. Being on cable, she could work from home without any difficulty. For those who had not got that facility, the school had set up study carrels, both in the main building and in outreach centres, which were open for 18 hours a day, and were always well used. She worked until 12:00, and then went back to the drama studio to meet Ellen for her weekly 'one-to-one'.

'Sit down, Judith. Coffee?'

'No thanks, Ellen. Whenever I'm trying to get something written, I drink far too much coffee. I'm awash. '

'I managed to reach that friend at Newcastle University. He is called Professor John Davies, and he'd be delighted to be your coach for the Restoration period study. As soon as you can, would you get in touch with him?'

'Oh, that's great. Thank you so much. I know his name from a book he wrote. He's brilliant. That's really good news.'

'Fine. I know you'll get a lot from his coaching. Generally, how are things going? I'm getting some good reports on your work in the crèche. Do you still enjoy it?

'Very much. You remember that I started to get interested in children's language development?'

Ellen nodded.

'Well, I'm putting the theory into perspective now, and really beginning to understand the underlying concepts so much better. And to get paid while I'm learning – that's a real bonus. I think, if the hospital placement comes up and fixes the spell on the children's ward, I'll be able to put together an interesting sound/word piece that might get me a learning credit.'

They chatted for a while about other aspects of Judith's work.

The headteacher left the canteen and went to the open-plan area used by a number of the administrative staff to pick up a lap-top before going to her tutorial group. Some time ago, when the centre was still about the business of deciding its basic values and ways of operating, there had been a staff meeting which, among a number of fairly important points, had one about office space. A fairly brave young teacher asked why the headteacher and deputies had offices of their own, and the rest of the staff had to muck in sharing a pretty scruffy staff room. There had been a hushed silence, and the head said, quietly, that a very important point had been made, and that an answer would be given at the next meeting.

At the next meeting the head had said that a lot of thinking had been devoted to the question, and no satisfactory reason for their having separate offices had been found. There was no moral or practical justification for the continuation of that practice. The head and deputies could hot-desk in the general administrative area when necessary, and borrow quiet rooms for interviews when needed. The signs came down that day.

The day was going to be a busy one for the head. She had planned to go to three of the outreach centres to talk to the staff and students there, and see how things were going. In this remote, mainly rural part of England, it was vital to have centres in the less accessible areas so that students who would otherwise be solely reliant on the screen and cable links, or would have very lengthy journeys, could meet with tutors and other students to talk over what they were doing, or, more generally, simply meet to have a chat. She also wanted to set aside a good hour that day to search the Internet to expand her list of coaches. Luckily, with a little persistence, it was still possible to find people who were expert in particular fields, and who would enjoy the challenge of enabling a student to grow in confidence and competence.

She decided to go to the office via the medical centre. Quite a few years ago, her predecessor had fought very hard to get the medical centre located on the college campus. The town council had decided that the old centre had to be replaced, and was looking for a new location. Andrew, the headteacher at the time, had argued hard and long for the centre's being located on the campus. His main theme was that as the college was rapidly becoming the focus for the community in so many ways, having the medical centre on campus was the logical extension. He also saw that as the college catered for more and more people, it made good sense to have medical facilities nearby.

The council eventually decided that the college was a good location, and the centre was built on the town side of the campus. Apart from its normal function, it had also acted as a powerful advertisement for the college. People coming to it for treatment would see Midtown Community Centre at work and play, would be able to pick up leaflets about courses that were available, and talk to one or two of the students who were doing some part-time work as receptionists or trainee nurses. An unexpected bonus was that it also became a learning centre for a number of students. In recent years, it had acquired a virtual operating theatre, so that the doctors could regularly update their techniques for the minor operations that they regularly carried out. The bonus was that a steady stream of students also used the facility, both those who were considering going into the medical profession, and those who were studying biology and needed to carry out dissections.

As she entered the centre, two students on work placement greeted her from the receptionist's area.

'Good morning, Ruth. Are you coming to see one of the doctors? Do you have an appointment?'

'Good morning, Sam and Helen. No, I'm not here to see a doctor. I think that there are two of us using the virtual theatre, and I wanted to see how things were going. Are you enjoying your placement?'

'Yes,' said Sam. 'It's very hard work keeping everything updated and in good order, but really interesting. You meet so many people. Yes, it's good. And yes, Leila and Peter are in there at the moment. I'm not too sure what they're doing though.'

'That's fine. I'll go and take a look. Hope you enjoy the rest of your placement.'

She went through to the back of the building to the room where the virtual operating theatre was housed. In the room, the two students had their helmets and gloves on and were clearly concentrating hard on some delicate movements. Also in the room was one of the doctors from the centre, keeping an eye on the equipment.

'Good morning, Ruth. Nice to see you. Just dropping in, or is this a medical visit?'

'No, just dropping in, Emma. What are those two doing this morning?'

'They're dissecting a rat, and they've got Professor Berg helping them.'

In the old days, because there was no alternative, real rats and frogs and so on were dissected in school laboratories and there had been an increasingly vociferous lobby against the practice, but until virtual reality had been established there had been no alternative. Now, there was no need to kill any animal, and the added bonus was that the students could do the dissection through a program at any time of their choosing, and with a leading teacher to guide them.

'Do you want me to stop them?' asked Emma.

'Oh no. They're totally absorbed, and I'd hate to interrupt. When they emerge, say hello for me, would you?'

'Fine, Ruth. Nice to have seen you.'

When she returned to the office, one of the assistants was waiting for her.

'I wonder if you would have a look at this. It's about the summer school. We seem to have expanded to the point where we are overbooked.'

Not too many years ago, there was the ludicrous situation that schools, expensive buildings with expensive resources, sat idle for about two months in the summer, and over weekends and for varying periods at Christmas and Easter. The old situation had changed and schools opened the year round, with the only total closure being for a few days at Christmas, and for three weeks in the summer to allow repairs and redecoration to take place. Students were able to choose at which periods of the year they would attend, and as long as the requisite amount of time was logged, it did not matter what blocks of time they chose. However, an increasing number of people were questioning whether there was any correlation between the time a student spent 'at school' and the subsequent outcomes. After all, it was accepted that people learnt different things at different rates, so why make everyone go to school for the same length of time? The important outcome was the demonstration of the learning, the showing that the student could use the knowledge he or she had acquired in a new situation. Simply adding up the time at a desk seemed a silly way to gauge a student's progress. Ruth was already bending the rules for a number of students, and had asked tutor teams to put together papers on the topic that could be discussed at the next general college meeting.

The summer school was a time for people coming to the North of England on holiday to combine tourism with a period of study, and it also gave regular students 'catch-up' time if they needed it, and remediation time if they were finding a certain area of their studies difficult. It was also a time for the college to make quite an addition to its budget, as it hired out areas and facilities for the many groups that came to perform. The most popular section of the summer school, though, was the performing arts section. Midtown would never be a real threat to the Edinburgh Festival, but it was becoming a place to which an increasing number of artists made their way, and the students, of course, benefited enormously and were contributors as well. Ruth and the town council were in the middle of talks about the possibility of a jointly funded conference centre, which would also be the focus point for an expanded summer festival.

'No, it's all right, Alan. While you were on holiday, I managed to get extra space in the Links hotel, and we might even be able to get some more room, if we need it, at the Metro in town.'

Ruth went to the admin area, and then on to the meeting room. She was going to have a working lunch with some headteachers from a group of schools in the United States who were visiting Midtown to see how the system worked. The schools had combined into the Expanding Schools Coalition, and wanted to link with Midtown as they thought that the aims and objectives of their group and of Midtown were highly compatible.

The four of them were already seated in the meeting room. Alan followed her in with sandwiches and coffee. After the usual introductions and formalities, one of the visitors asked Ruth if, in a few words, she could sum up the philosophy of Midtown, and the main ways in which it worked.

'Yes, certainly,' Ruth said. 'But it will have to be brief, as I am due at an out-reach centre very soon. In any case, I think that seeing and hearing and talking to the people in the college are the best ways of getting to know what we are about. I have arranged for four students to pick you up here after you have finished your lunch, and they will be your guides for as long as you like. I suggest that we meet at your hotel at around seven, and we'll have dinner together. We can talk as long as you like then. Does that suit?'

They nodded.

'Fine. Well, in brief, the first and foremost principle is that the whole place is designed to help people learn – and I do mean everyone. We try to ensure that there are no sacred cows, no historical hangups, no "we've always done it this way" blockages that get in the way of learning. Every structure, every routine, every action is closely scrutinised, and there is one question that is always asked: "Does this, whatever it is, actually help someone to learn, and not hinder someone else?"

'Second, we try very hard indeed to remember all the time that at the heart of the college must be relationships. In the past, I think that too often we allowed the content of the curriculum to dominate; you used to hear people talking about "having to get through the material – we've got so much to get through". We used to forget that the important thing was not the content but the people involved. Now we spend a tremendous amount of time trying to ensure that the relationships are right, that there is time for people to talk and listen and get to be at ease with each other. That's why we put a prime importance on the tutorial set-up. And if we find that a student and a teacher or coach or tutor just can't get on, then we don't blame anyone or try to force the issue; we just change the combination.

'Third, as I said, everyone is a learner. A teacher or a secretary or a business manager or a caretaker, or a headteacher for that matter, who has stopped learning is no use to us.

'Now those two demands – relationships being the most important factor, and everyone being a learner – make for uncertainty. People interacting with each other, and changing through their learning, do not lead to placid certainties. There is volatility, bubble, uncertainty – white-water rafting rather than punting on a shallow lake. My job is to help keep the whole thing careering along more or less in the right direction, and at times it is very demanding and exhausting. But I'd hate to be the head of one of those schools where everything was predictable, and ordered and quiet and staid. Bored children and boring teachers! Of course, one of the unpredictables is not knowing where a student is going to end up. There is enormous excitement in trying to keep up with someone who is learning at such a clip that he or she is running way ahead of you. All you can do is encourage and cheer – but there is no question of controlling. Marvellous.

'Fourth, we try very hard to make sure that all students demonstrate that they have achieved an applicable outcome. We keep the outcomes as flexible as we possibly can, but in one way or another the outcome must show that whatever knowledge a student has acquired, it can be demonstrated and used in imaginative and resourceful ways. It goes without saying that all the activities in the place – learning, coaching, mentoring, teaching – all are designed to ensure that the student has really learned something and then can choose the best way and time to demonstrate that learning.

'We monitor the learning process and progress of each individual as closely as possible, to ensure that the learning style and rate are matched by the appropriate range of materials and activities, and that there is a constant reiteration of the high expectations that we have of each other. Finally, we provide immediate remediation for students who have gaps and slow patches. I suppose that the guiding principle is that we believe everyone can learn, and we, and they, have to use our imaginations to find the best way for that learning to take place, and for a range of outcomes that suit the individual.

'Before I finish, just a word about how we got to the type of place that you are going to tour very soon. I suppose that the main feature which differentiates us from the traditional school of the twentieth century is that the relative power of the three points of the triangle have altered, and altered fundamentally. The three points are student, teacher and information. Twenty years ago, for all sorts of reasons that we won't go into now, the most powerful point was the teacher. Teachers and other adults, like the ruling political party, controlled the information, through selecting the textbook or through the National Curriculum which was in place then, or through the overall funding, or through the timing of the library's opening, or through the length of time allocated to a subject, or through the prevailing culture, and so on and on. The students were the least powerful. They had to conform if they wanted the right credentials at the end of the process, and they had to fit into the procrustean bed which we called schooling. They also had to fit in with a system that favoured the two intelligences which, in a self-perpetuating way, had been in favour for years – the verbal and the logico-scientific.

'Once we had the technological breakthrough which released information, and students could access what they wanted, when they wanted it and where they wanted it, then the power relationships also changed, and freed up the system marvellously. That, and the recognition that we have seven or nine intelligences, and suddenly we had a new set of priorities, and a whole new view of what we mean by a school.

'There!' she smiled. 'As far as potted philosophies go, that wasn't bad. Now, the students are waiting outside. Go and see if we put into practice what we preach. I really hope you enjoy yourselves. See you at dinner.'

The first group that one of the visitors joined was just beginning an English seminar. There were fifteen in the group, of whom six were adults. The remainder were of different ages from 15 to 18. The teacher was Simon.

'Right. The pattern for the next hour and a half is the usual one. I want you to study some scenes from the CD-Roms, and then we'll discuss what you think about them.' He turned to the visitor and explained that the group was studying *Hamlet*.

'There are three versions of the same scene,' he told them. 'It is the scene before the play-within-the-play when Hamlet and Ophelia have that conversation that is so problematic. We were looking at it yesterday, and could not decide what tone we would adopt were we to be playing Ophelia. In the scenes that they are going to watch in a moment they will see the same two actors in each, but in one Ophelia is a straight county type, innocent, open, without guile. In the next, she's a really rather lewd tart – there is nothing innocent about her at all, and both she and Hamlet know this. Third, she is flirty and joking, but nothing much more than that. The idea is that they will watch them very carefully, and then try to decide which portrait fits in best with the rest of the play.'

He turned to the group. 'When you've finished, together we'll try, yet again, to decide which version we believe in.' The group swivelled their chairs round to the individual screens, put on their headphones and started to watch the scene.

Simon turned back to the visitor.

'You see, the great advantage we have over the sort of teaching we had years ago is that we can watch the play that we're studying played by top actors, we can watch workshops by those actors, we can hold a frame to study the body language and set it against the words being spoken, we can go back to a scene as many times as we want – the whole system is so flexible and gives the students real control. Above anything else, of course, it means that the students are studying a play, and not a text. You won't see it this afternoon, unfortunately, but later this week we'll go to the drama studio, and we'll act this scene, record it on disc, and then we can compare and contrast.'

Judith walked over to room 18, where she was to meet her buddy. Many of the older students volunteered to meet on a weekly basis with a younger student as part of the coaching and mentoring programme. She liked Ahmed enormously, and the two of them looked forward to their weekly meeting. He had brought with him the book he was reading at the time, and they started off by him reading a passage.

'That's great,' said Judith. 'Not a single mistake. But your voice is still pretty flat. You don't sound as if you're really involved with what you're reading.'

'I'm not,' said Ahmed with a grin. 'It's a very boring book. I really don't like books much anyway. The electrobook – now that's different. I can do something with that. But just this flat old thing – I don't like it. You promised to tell me a story. Go on – tell me a story. One of those from long, long ago about the giants that used to live around here.'

Judith grinned back. 'You're a great one at getting your own way, aren't you?'

In fact, she enjoyed this part of the session as she could practise what she was good at, and she could see over the weeks that Ahmed was developing a real love of stories and poems, and his English tutor said that his own story-telling was really improving. She struck a suitable pose, Ahmed giggled, and then she was off.

One of the visitors was talking earnestly to Lata, his guide.

'What baffles me is how anyone knows what on earth is going on, what anyone is doing, or not doing. I mean – look at all this.'

They were standing in the middle of the quadrangle. It was about four o'clock, and there was a considerable movement of students. For some it was the end of the time that they spent in the building, and they were off home, or to one of the learning centres that had been set up in two parts of the town and in half-a-dozen of the surrounding villages. No student was going to be disadvantaged by not being able to afford a PC and the cable link. Others were going to the playing fields at the back of the main building, and a group was gathering outside the drama studio waiting to start rehearsal for the musical that was to be one of the highlights of the summer school. There were also students in ones and twos going to see a tutor, join a subject group or going to one of the study carrels in the area over the crèche or to the cafeteria.

'I mean – just look. There must be hundreds of people coming and going at all sorts of times, and not just here but in other parts of the town and even further away. How is it all controlled? It looks like choas to me.'

'"Controlled" is not the right word,' Lata said. 'That sounds too much like an army. We base so much of what we do on the tutor system. Over the years, the tutor gets to know us, and we get to know our tutor, really well. We build up a lot of trust between us. The tutor's job is to make sure that we can get on with our learning in ways that make sense to us, and she or he does everything possible to help us. It's that regular meeting every morning with the group, and then the weekly one-to-one that keeps the whole thing moving along. It isn't chaos.' She paused, and smiled as she looked at the crowds of people moving around the campus.

'It works really well, and we don't get wound up about it. "Relaxed purposefulness" – I'm quoting Ruth. Of course, computers help. They take the hassle out of things. Tutors can really concentrate on us, and not bother with "administrivia" as my tutor likes to call it. As you come onto the campus or go into any of the outreach centres, you log on through the palm-swipe screen. That registers that you are here, and if a tutor wants to talk with you, then she or he could tell you were somewhere around and could put a message out for you. Then every time you start work on anything to do with your studies, you enter your name and your student number and the computer logs you on and records what you are doing, and records any assessments that it gives or that your teacher gives, or that you give yourself. If you are doing some work-shadowing or some time out on a field trip, then again you log on at the beginning and the end and the computer records it all. And, of course, everything you do that you want to keep as a record of progress and because you're proud of it, that goes onto the computer and your tutor can have a look at it, or listen to it. I've got some video of a dance sequence that I choreographed, and some music that my group played, and that is part of my project on the history of Leicester in the 1950s. As you progress, the computer is building up a record of achievement, and then when you're ready it is transferred to CD, and there you have it – my record in colour, with the music and art that I've done – the lot. And, of course, the computer programs are always pushing you on. "Have you thought of this? Well done; now you are ready to do. . . You seem to be good at x; here is an extended problem." They really never let up.

'But the mechanical part is all in the background. You don't really notice it after a while. The heart of it all is you and your tutor.'

'But what if you don't get on, if you don't like each other?' the visitor interrupted. 'Then what?'

'Then you put in a request to the tutor team for a transfer, and you get one.' She looked rather surprised at the question. 'It is the tutor who, with help from other teachers and coaches, really guides you, sees that you keep up to what both of you know you can do. I call mine "The Kindly Prod".'

'It still seems to me that it all looks too casual, too relaxed. Do you really study hard? Now, don't get me wrong. I'm not trying to suggest that you don't work hard, but I want to sell this back in the States, so I need all the good answers that you can give.'

Lata smiled. 'No, I understand. That's fine. I've often heard my parents and grandparents talk about what it was like when they went to school. It doesn't seem to me that they enjoyed it much. It seems that it was terribly regimented, and there was an awful lot of sitting in a classroom listening to the teacher. Very boring. And all much of a muchness – what you did in one lesson in this subject was much like what you did in another on that subject. I think that our work is so much more exciting. Let me give you an example. If I have a paper to do on a topic, let's say that history project on Leicester, I don't have just one or two textbooks to read, or a worksheet from the teacher and then four or five books from the library, if I can get them. I have masses of material, original letters and diaries, newspapers, and the music and songs, and pictures of the clothes and recipes of what people ate, and their bills for holidays, and, and, and. There is just such a mass. But what I'm doing is sifting first-hand evidence. I'm a real historian, not just someone merely learning about history. And that's really exciting. It means that I have to have a system, a system for learning, really. It seems to me that my parents just learned how to be taught. I've had to learn how to learn. Of course, my tutor and coach are both marvellous and they help, but there is a lot more that is for me to do.'

The tutor team started its meeting at 4:30. The chair and leader for the month was Sean.

'Right, there are only two topics that we all need to discuss, and one that I'd like to talk to you about, Jane, so the meeting shouldn't take long. The first item is that by the next meeting we should all have our learning plan in the system and each have read all the others so that we can ask questions, comment – you know, the usual scrutiny. So I think we should have them available on screen within the next two weeks.'

Everyone, from the youngest child to the oldest adult who used the campus, had a learning plan. For the younger child, the plan might extend only over the next few days, but for the older students the plan could cover the next six or more months. The idea was that the student and his or her tutor would sketch out the topic and the pattern of study and the outcomes that could be expected, and then monitor progress against that template. Similarly, every adult that worked in Midtown Community Centre also had a learning plan; another slogan of the first head of the centre, and one echoed by the present incumbent, was: 'In a learning community, everyone learns.' Of course, the network of coaches was also used to help with the teachers' learning plans. At first there had been no outside bodies which could validate much of the learning, but gradually the Accreditation Centres widened their remit so that no matter what the person's age, and no matter what the topic learnt, everyone could have that learning accredited. These outside agencies were vital as they gave value to the learning, and meant that, when it was necessary, the public could have faith in the qualifications gained.

'Second – we've got a problem with Darren. In very brief terms, he says that he wants to learn Spanish, and I'm certain that he is being truthful. He seems genuinely fascinated by the place, and its music. But, when he's with Maria he drives her mad; he just can't sit still and talk to her or read to her or listen to her. He's jiggling about all the time, gets up to walk about, always on the move or wanting to be. He's OK studying on his own, but of course he needs the one-to-one talks and so on to get his spoken language up to scratch. What's to be done? I've had a number of chats with him, and he doesn't mean to be a pest or to be rude. But things are not going well. Any ideas?'

'Well,' said Simon, 'I think that I might have an idea. I know you'll tell me if I am completely mad. Darren is a very physical boy, and a damned good athlete. His specialism is fell running, and you know what sort of physical and mental determination that takes. How about if we make sure that Darren has his training, then a break for a shower and to get his breath back, and then he goes to Maria? He'll be physically pretty well exhausted, and he may well find it easier to sit and talk to Maria in a way that keeps her sane, and him able to concentrate. What do you think?'

'I like it very much. Let's have a look at their schedules and see how we can make everything fit in. OK, that's great. Nothing else of importance, and we've all got lots to do. Thanks for coming. Jane, could we have a very brief word, please? Before you came up to this part of the world and started teaching, you were an office manager, weren't you?'

'That's right. I ran the office of a large medical practice in North London. Why?'

'Well, the person who was tutor for the office people here has left, and it seemed to me that it would be a good idea, if we possibly could, to have someone as their tutor who understood their work and the pressures and so on. You'd also know what sorts of career portfolios they should be putting together. Would you like to take it on?'

'Yes, I would very much. Thank you.'

Ruth had returned from her visits to the outreach centres and was talking to the Business Manager.

'Altogether a very worthwhile trip. And I was so pleased that you let me see a copy of that letter that Alastair was thinking of sending out.'

'Did you sort it out with him?' asked Savita.

'Yes, and it was really a good growth point. I could understand the motivation behind the idea – we are short of money, lighting and heating cost money and it stays dark for a long time and gets very cold up here in the winter, so let's stay within budget by opening later and closing earlier. Very logical.'

'So how did you deal with it?'

'Probably in a way that will not sit easily with you. Question: what, Alistair, is your main role here; indeed, what is the role of these outreach centres and of Midtown as a whole? Is it to keep within a budget?'

'Oh, really Ruth!' exploded Savita. 'That's not fair. You know that we have to keep within a budget, otherwise we can't do all the things that we want to do.'

Ruth grinned. 'Yes I know, and you know that I know. But I was trying to get him to take a particular point. Let me continue. His answer was much as yours; the main purpose is to help people learn, but if we run out of money we won't be able to, and he was trying to save money. Question: how can you save money, and still open the same hours? – and, of course, you know how many people use Alistair's centre. It would be a great loss for a lot of people to keep it closed for an extra three hours a day. So he thought for a while, and then said that he could reduce the heating. I agreed and said that a notice asking people to bring an extra sweater might be a good idea. But that would not be enough. He thought a bit more, and then said that up to now he had been allowing people to brew up free of charge, and added that it did seem a bit odd that money that might go to computer time or cable charges went into brewing up pots of tea. I agreed, and said that he needed to get in touch with you and sort out a reasonable charge. He took the point in the end that what we always do is search our hardest, using every ounce of imagination, in order to protect the core. Before I left he had come up with three more really good ideas. Mission accomplished – and he's learning about budgets. You might look pleased, Savita.'

'Oh, I am really; you know I am. I'm trying to think of a way of calculating the cost of the electricity for a pot of tea. New one for me.'

'Learning, always learning.' Ruth laughed, and went into her office to get ready for the evening with the visitors.

Judith went to the crèche for a final tidying up, and for a last check to see if there were any messages on her lap-top. Her French teacher had gone through the paper and had sent thanks and congratulations. He thought that the section on the rise of regionalism was most important and suggested getting in touch with a friend at the University of Toulouse to get some information on the Occitaine. He warned Judith that the French Professor's English was not very good, so she would have to practise her conversational French as well as learn about the Occitaine decentralisation movement. Judith sighed. There was one more message. The placement in the city hospital had been agreed, so she wrote herself a reminder to talk to the tutor the next morning to get time out.

She packed up, locked the door, and went through the gates, pressing her palm on the screen to let the computer know that she was signing off for the day. It had been a long day, but all in all, a pretty good one.

2

■ ■ ■

An Overview

As the world becomes more interconnected and business becomes more complex and dynamic, work must become more 'learningful'. It is no longer sufficient to have one person learning for the organisation, a Ford or a Sloan or a Watson. It's just not possible any longer to 'figure it out' from the top, and have everyone else following the 'grand strategist'. The organisations that will truly excel in the future will be the organisations that discover how to tap people's commitment and capacity to learn at all levels in an organisation. (Peter Senge, *The Fifth Discipline* (p 4))

One of the problems with looking into a new world and trying to describe what is there is that you have to use the language of the old. Let us give you an example. In your day-to-day working life, you use a computer in your work as an engineer. You are given the chance to use a time machine to visit your great grandfather who lived in the middle of the nineteenth century. Inevitably, he will ask you what you do, and you try to explain what a computer is. There is no chance of any real understanding between the two of you, because the concepts underpinning the languages that you each have are mutually exclusive. As you try even harder to convey your meanings, the chances are that the words you use will set off reactions and memories that will inevitably take him further and further away from understanding you. You would sound to him as if you indulged in gazing at runes, or in some other black art.

The language we use

In this book we want to try to describe what is in part a new approach to education, a new way of thinking about schools and learning, and what is at the same time an updating and recasting of a philosophical attitude to learning and a way of looking at the world that goes back to Aristotle. We believe that the world of learning is on the threshold of a paradigm shift, because the paradigm we have been using for the last three hundred years, based on a world view emanating from Descartes ('I think, therefore I am'), the Age of Enlightenment and Newtonian science, is no longer viable. However, we are forced to use the language of the old paradigm to try to outline the new.

The language includes the words 'school', 'management', 'leadership', 'education', 'learning', 'teaching'. All of us have employed these words for as long as we can remember, not only to discuss the schooling and education of ourselves, and then of our children and pupils, but also, by implication, to indicate a particular way of looking at society. The 'language game' of this part of our world carries with it a value system so that when, in this book, we try to change the meaning of the word, as we will with those words just listed and many more, we know that we are trying to change the value system of our readers. At the very least, we will be hoping that you will be tolerant enough to allow our set of values to run in parallel alongside yours for the time you are reading the book. Which set of values eventually predominates will be, in part, a measure of the success of this book.

Our plea at this early stage, therefore, is for you to stay with us long enough to become aware of the new set of rules and values and meanings that we are using. We hope to show a logically coherent world through our language and argument.

Education as symbol

It has been argued by many writers that education is in no small measure about symbolic knowledge which is important, not because of any use to which the learner can put it, but because possession of that knowledge is seen by society as a necessary passport to higher education or to decent employment – a necessary filter, in other words. For example, Latin was once the passport to almost every university course, even though it had no direct application; a Classics degree was the entrée to a career in the Colonial Office, not because such a degree helped you in your post as District Commissioner in East Africa, but because possession of such a degree meant that you had been to the right school and university, and belonged, therefore, to the ruling class. We will argue later that much of the National Curriculum (NC) is there as symbol. We will also argue that much of the NC, and its attendant assessment procedures and the implications for learning which arise from those assessments, are reifications of social practice as opposed to being based on a logically derived philosophy of learning.

We will be using the arguments of Popper (1960) to show the weak foundations of the NC and of one of its arms, Ofsted. In essence, Popper shows that a statement which cannot be proved false cannot, equally, be proved true. An assertion that the United Kingdom is in moral decline cannot be proved false as there are no hard and fast measurements against which the present state of morality can be measured and compared. Both the National Curriculum and Ofsted are based on such assertions. They deal, in the main, with symbolic knowledge, and are doctrinaire products of a particular ideology.

Education versus schooling

A further problem facing anyone writing about a new approach to schools and education is that education and schooling have been, and still are, confused, the latter being seen as an essential in achieving the former. There is a certain expectation that the school will produce young people who conform, in the main, to the current societal norms. A school that produced children that were in rebellion would be seen at best as a failure, at worst as dangerous. There is, in some popular notions about what schools should be, more than a touch of the carceral.

The educated person

There are, however, only the most tenuous links between 'being educated' and 'being schooled'. It is necessary, therefore, to be very clear about what is meant by the term 'an educated person'. The use of the past participle makes it very important to attempt a definition as the participle suggests that there is a terminal point in the business of being educated, and that once there, a person can rest secure in the knowledge that education is now over. This is a mistake. An educated person is one who never stops learning, one whose curiosity perpetually drives them on to find out more, one for whom learning is as essential as eating and breathing. There are other characteristics, all of which are attributes of this passion for learning, such as tentativeness, openness to discussion, a capacity for wonder. Certainly being educated has nothing to do with the 'Brain of Britain' or 'Mastermind' quiz shows. In Chapter 4 there is an analysis of learning, but at this point it is enough to give a taxonomy of learning, and stress that it is the fourth and fifth types of learning that underpin the idea of the educated person as one who is always learning.

1 *Learning as memorisation.* Some of such memorisation is important (e.g. the times tables, the rules of spelling) as the rules memorised enable higher functions to be undertaken without conscious thought as to the foundation activities. Some memorisation, however, is important only until the next test or examination, and the material memorised can be, and indeed often is, discarded as soon as the test is over. We may therefore divide memorisation

into functional memorisation, and shallow memorisation or shallow learning.

2 *Learning as a quantitative increase in our knowledge on a topic.* If I am becoming interested in gardening, for example, by experience, by talking to other gardeners and reading books and magazines on the subject, and, of course, by gardening, I increase the body of knowledge that I have on the subject.

3 *Learning as the creation of personal meaning.* From our earliest conscious moment, we are learning about the people and things around us – what is safe and trustworthy and what is not, what is warm and what is repellent, and so on – because without this learning we cannot make sense of the world in which we live.

4 *Learning which results in the creation of our reality.* As a continuation of 3 above, from the learning about the people and things around us we create our sense of reality, which is shifting and uncertain over time, but which at any given moment allows us to know our world and function in it.

5 *Learning which results in our changing as a person.* This learning, deep learning, is what occurs when a new idea, a new perception, a new grasp on a topic fundamentally alters the way we are, the way we behave.

Naturally, such a listing is, to a degree, arbitrary as one type of learning melds into another without perceptible break, but it is useful nonetheless in that it highlights the predominant types of learning favoured in schools and by most politicians.

It follows from the above that what we are concerned with in this book is the fifth type of learning. Another way of putting it is to say that we see the major end purpose of education as being concerned with enabling people to change, to construct their own reality through being able thoroughly to analyse the evidence they encounter, and thereby be able to make informed choices based on a clear ethical base. We see the development of the mind as the overriding purpose of education.

Mind and intelligence

It is necessary to make a very clear distinction between the word 'mind' as it is used in this book, and the word 'intelligence' as it used in day-to-day speech, and in such phrases as 'intelligence test' and 'intelligent quotient'. In such phrases and usages there is the implicit and sometimes explicit assumption that intelligence is a fixed quantity, and the amount possessed by a person can be quantified and then plotted on a graph. That graph can then be used to place the person on a curve, and the position having been plotted, the next assumption made is that a meaningful and lasting statement has been made about the person's capabilities. Further, and arising from the sorts of tests that are administered to establish the intelligence rating of the person, there is the assumption that some sorts of knowledge are culturally more important than other sorts of knowledge. This hierarchy leads on to two further assumptions: first, that there is an ordered sequence to the learning that children must accomplish, and second that learning which can be displayed through written tests is of a higher order than that which can be displayed through a practical demonstration.

By focusing on 'mind', we mean to emphasise that there is in every person a widespread capacity for thoughtfulness, and that according to circumstances and experiences, and the range of resources brought to bear, people's abilities can be changed. There are, as Howard Gardner (1993) so eloquently demonstrates, multiple intelligences, and these intelligences require a wide variety of opportunities to flourish and to be demonstrated. In the main, our schools focus on two intelligences – linguistic intelligence and mathematical-scientific or logical intelligence. Our schools, and the national assessment system, give most importance to tests which are within the boundaries of those two intelligences. There is a circularity about such input and testing: children learn most of the content of the curriculum through the media of the written word, in the textbooks, worksheets and notes, and of the spoken word, mostly in the form of question-and-answer sessions. The tests which attempt to establish how much of this material has been learnt are administered mainly through one medium – a written answer in response to the written question; the question is, in the main, a demand for demonstration of memory rather than a demand for the application of a concept or piece of information to a totally new situation. It is clear, however, that learning is best measured when it can be applied to situations and problems hitherto unmet. Furthermore, the means by which the student demonstrates that learning should be negotiated between the teacher and the student, and should include as wide a range of media as is needed to encompass the student's depth and breadth of learning.

Non-linear learning

There are three other points that need to be made briefly, and then developed in Chapter 4. First, learning does not follow a neat sequence, but is dependent on qualitative understanding. Much of the National Curriculum, and the attendant work schemes, have as their underpinnings an implicit or explicit sequence. Obviously, in some instances a student must learn A before being able to go on to B. However, in many cases no one can mandate what the outcome of learning A might be; it could lead to B, but equally it could lead to K or X, and then return, via N and F, to B. Neat sequences are in the country of the bureaucrat, not of the learner.

Learning as a social activity

Second, learning is a social activity. We learn by talking together, doing things together; that much is accepted. More important, however, is the fact that learning does not occur as the result of a one-way 'input'. What I learn is a result of the interactions that arise when I, the teacher, the material, colleagues and friends, and the circumstances in which the other items come together and interact.

Learning and resources

Finally, thinking and learning do not occur in a vacuum, but when there are resources to stimulate and sustain them. The notion that the state of the building, the quantity and state of the books, and the numbers in the classroom are all merely peripheral to learning shows a fine disregard for what learning really is. If one follows the idea that learning is a direct result of a unilinear input from the teacher, then resources, apart from a minimum of heat and light, are probably irrelevant. If, on the other hand, one believes that a child's mind can expand indefinitely if given the right food, then the circumstances, the ambience, into which we put that child are all-important.

Learning for collaboration and autonomy

To return to the theme of being 'educated'. Being educated is being able to make decisions based on a balanced mixture of emotions and intellects, and being able to draw on a range of experiences which cumulatively gives the individual a range of choices. It follows, therefore, that from as early an age as practical, pupils will be helped to make decisions about their learning, with the aim of making them autonomous in their decision-making as soon as possible. Children do not learn to make decisions unless they make decisions. Further, the idea, touched on above, that learning is a social activity, and that collaborative learning needs to be a part of every child's experience, fits well with the emphasis on working in teams which, more and more, is the approach favoured by business and industry.

In addition, the educated person is the person who can see connections between and among seemingly disparate items, and by so seeing, find ways through to solutions when the one who thinks only in a linear fashion becomes increasingly bogged down. Collaborative learning, therefore, and learning which is not contained within artificial boundaries – the approach that is signalled by such comments as 'this is a Geography lesson; we cannot discuss that topic as it's clearly History; you cannot possibly do B before you have thoroughly covered A' – must be key features in our ideal education system. At present, our schools emphasise linearity and atomisation, attributes that are actually inimical to learning, and thus to survival in the world in which our children are going to live.

Deep learning

We also stress that learning must have a consequence for the learner. By 'consequence' we mean that by learning x, the learner will see the world in a slightly different way, will alter his or her behaviour or attitude in some way. If the 'learning' that has taken place is merely capable of being reproduced at some later date in answer to the demands of some form of assessment which replicates the original problem and the context for that problem, then what is being learnt is 'shallow learning' only. 'Deep learning', as we will demonstrate in Chapter 4, results in a change of behaviour, a change in the way the learner sees the world, a change in the reality which that learner is continuously creating.

The ethics of individualism

It is important to stress at this stage the moral purpose that is true education. The morality emerges from the tensions inherent in the contrary pulls of individualism and social determinism. Individualism must be dominant, otherwise there is a gradual but steady drift to totalitarianism; however, that individualism must be rooted in a freely accepted ethic, otherwise there is the certainty of selfishness. Individualism, it must be stressed, is not necessarily about the gratification of individual desires; rather it is about the continuous growth of the individual so that at all points in life, he or she can make meanings from what is happening around them. Thomas Greenfield (Greenfield and Ribbins, 1993) said that meaning is possible only in individual terms and through individual experience. Our schools are posited on the concept that the teacher can convey meaning to the child, and that there is a centrally accepted and sanctioned set of meanings that need to be handed over to the child and absorbed. Such is not the case. Each individual creates his or her meaning from the raw material of experience, the discipline of a subject area, from interactions with others. As the individual exists among others, is a social animal, then the meanings must reflect the claims and needs of the community, and be interpreted by the community. It must not be thought that such an emphasis on individualism is an argument for rampant egoism; egoism has no place in the interpretative community that is the ideal society.

Without the fullest development of the individual there can be no community. With partially developed individuals there can be regimentation, there can be compliance, there can be a neat and tidy order. A properly functioning community, however, demands that each member be an autonomous individual, learning, developing, changing, expanding. Such individuals can establish an interpretative community which voluntarily and through never-ending discussion and articulation of ideas, and through an acceptance of those fundamental ethics that are common to all major religions and philosophies, establishes the norms and mores which all in the community will understand. Such a community is not easily governed; it is argumentative, assertive, changing. It does not accept rules from a hierarchy; indeed it does not accept the idea of a hierarchy. But it is not, as some would try to argue, chaotic, and because chaotic, undesirable. A school which truly established itself as an interpretative community would have no need of a supervisory educational quango, an inspectorate demanding compliance with a National Curriculum, nationally ordained tests, inspections and the like. The community of the school would, for itself, and with critical friends, hammer out what a 'good education' meant, and would have no need of a remote, self-appointed hierarchy to make that meaning for it. In such a school, the main emphasis would be on the steady growth of each person in it towards being an autonomous learner, able to take part in and contribute to the community. It is that ability to participate in the creating and sustenance of a community that is the moral imperative for schools. Schools, if they are to be about the business of education and not schooling, need to break away from the dependency culture that the 'nanny State' wishes to preserve.

Knowledge and control

One of the manifestations of the quango's control is the expressed notion that it has the monopoly over the 'reality' that children must accept. Such an imposed 'reality' manifests itself in such comments as: 'This is the knowledge, the content that you require to function in the type of society that we think you need.' In fact, Her Majesty's Chief Inspector of Schools said in a talk given in February 1997 (Woodhead, 1997): 'If the pupil is to be initiated into this body of knowledge, then he [sic] must *submit* himself to the teacher's greater understanding.' And later in the same speech, he said: '. . . we have lost sight of the concept of education as a transaction bewteen the generations in which the young are initiated into those aspects of *our* culture which *we* deem to be worth preserving.' (Our emphases).

By controlling what is meant by the word 'knowledge', and by deliberately confusing 'knowledge' with 'information', the quango and its political bosses attempt to control the people. If I, as one of the people at the top of this hierarchy, can obtain compliance or acceptance from you as to what constitutes knowledge, then I have the power to decide on what you learn, how you learn it and how you demonstrate that learning. I have, in large measure, control over you as a person because I can negate, ridicule or outlaw anything that falls outside what I have decided is 'knowledge'. For the government, schooling is one of the prime levers it has to maintain control, and therefore it busies itself about the setting of the boundaries of knowledge, and the limits within which schools can operate. However, the hierarchy now faces a very considerable problem. Information is expanding exponentially; it is said that information doubles every four years. Because of IT, no government can be 'in control' of information nor of its growth. In order to say that 'this constitutes what we have decided you need to know', the quango has to exclude increasingly large swathes of information; it has to be careless with the truth by pretending that it can have a monopoly on what is or is not germane to our children's education. The quango is, in fact, out of control; by pretending that it can be in control it demonstrates blind arrogance.

There is, however, the contrary philosophy, one that has attached to it the ugly word 'subsidiarity'. It is a term inherent in the Constitution of the United States of America, which says, in effect, that only those powers stated in the Constitution as belonging to central government can be wielded by central government. Everything not so listed is in the power of the individual states. Such a notion of subsidiarity needs to be applied to education. The power to decide what is knowledge, the power to make meaning, must rest primarily with the individual, and with a group of individuals who, in freedom and trust, choose to create a community. It cannot rest with central government.

Learning and structures

It follows from the above argument that learning is both an individual and a collective discipline, and therefore that school management is in part about enabling and showing the learner how to be individually disciplined within an agreed contract, and how the learner can combine with the collective to widen everyone's ability to learn. What is at the heart of this argument is the learning. The management structures and functions must have learning as their base and *raison d'être*. In other words, form follows function, or structure follows strategy. What has been the case, very largely, in the past has been that the structure of management has tended to be constructed with the whole institution in mind – how a school of 100 adults and 1000 pupils can be managed most efficiently. The structures did not look to the best interests of the individual learner.

Schools in the 1960s and 1970s grew rapidly in size and complexity. Business and commerce were looked to for management solutions, but unfortunately the systems that were then current were hierarchical and bureaucratic. It was the bureaucratic element that was so inimical to schools' real function. The main feature of a bureaucracy is that it breaks down the work to the smallest component part, and each part is doled out to a worker. The worker is relieved of the responsibility for seeing the linkage with other parts of the work, and, in theory, through repeating the same small task day in and day out, will become proficient. So it was with schools. The task of the school was broken into the 'academic' part and the 'pastoral' part. The 'academic' part was then further reduced, so that this teacher was responsible for the teaching of English to these five groups, but never saw them using the language in, say, science. That teacher was responsible for constructing the timetable, but never asked if the resultant grid helped that individual learn to his or her maximum. Another teacher was the 'line manager' for a group of heads of department, but he or she did not know from first-hand evidence what the received curriculum was for any individual child. No one could have a holistic knowledge of the individual child, and the child was never enabled to see the wholeness of his or her education.

The irony is that having imported these organisations from commerce, schools are, in the main, still stuck with them when successful businesses all over the world have jettisoned them. Businesses have changed partly because middle managers can be replaced by software, which is faster and more reliable, and partly because bureaucracies cannot adapt quickly enough to change, and partly because it was found that people worked infinitely better when they saw themselves as part of the whole picture. A further major problem with that outmoded form of organisation is that it can lead to managerialism, that disease which strikes organisations and makes them believe that keeping the machine moving is at least as important as knowing where it is moving to and for what purpose.

If we now see the overriding need as being the enablement and encouragement of the individual to learn, then it follows that the management structure has to be alongside the learner, and not looking down from a height: 'There is nothing more important to an individual committed to his or her own growth than a supportive environment' (Senge, 1993, p 173).

The argument that we are putting forward, and which will be fleshed out in subsequent chapters, is that the organisation of an educational institution must be based on the superordinate rights of the individual learner. In case that statement sounds like a return to the days of Tyndale, let us very firmly point to what we have said above – that learning arises out of discipline; that the discipline is that of the interpretative community; that in the early stages of the development of a learner that discipline will be coming from outside the learner, but that as time passes the aim is to decrease the external discipline and increase the internal; that the medium- and longer-term objective is the autonomous learner.

Once we accept that fundamental idea, that of the individual learner being the starting point for the form of the organisation, then certain other imperatives follow. We need to find ways in which to legitimate the management of schools, and the legitimation comes from the extent to which the individual child and adult in that institution are enabled and encouraged to learn. We look, therefore, for the closest fit between intention and outcome; we look for consistency, match, congruity. The intention is that the child will be enabled to make informed choices. In Chapter 6 we shall analyse the sort of leadership required to create the organisation which enables deep learning to occur.

At present, there are many features of school organisation which exist in order that teaching can take place. We want to suggest ways in which the organisation needs to be based on the needs of the learner. Up to now, the emphasis on the teacher has been inevitable. The role of the teacher has been to manage the available information in such a way that groups of children could best assimilate it and then reproduce it in a manner which was susceptible to mass marking. The information that children needed as the building bricks has been in comparatively short supply: there is a limit to the number of textbooks that can be bought and used; there is a limit to the size and opening hours of the library; there is a need, when dealing with groups of 24 or 30 children, to make learning sequential and controlled. The arrival of IT, however, has begun to alter the relative importance of the three parts of the triangle – learner, information, teacher. With information becoming cheaper and available at any time, and becoming portable and unbounded by traditional labels, we see the teacher as becoming increasingly the coach or mentor as the child grows into being an autonomous learner.

At present, we create timetables which are designed to enable adults to teach. We never ask of a particular child whether he or she learns English better if that lesson is preceded by French and followed by Spanish, or whether he or she would do better to have the English preceded by PE and followed by drama. We frequently write, in the school's aims and objectives, about fulfilling 'each child's *individual* needs', but then for the majority of the time we deal with the children in groups. Lessons are on average 40 minutes long, but we do not know which of our children learn most easily, or with the greatest difficulty, in that time slot. We, or rather the NC, prescribe the content to be studied, but we do not, or cannot at the moment, look to see if other content, or linkages of content, would help that child learn faster and more comfortably. Without exaggerating too much, there is something of the Procrustean bed about our schools; some children are left disabled by being hacked about to fit the curriculum; some are 'stretched' to take up the available space; others, less malleable or thought less worthy of treatment, never fit and are labelled as having 'Special Educational Needs'. What we will be showing in Chapter 3 is that, *inter alia*, the arrival of IT can free us from many of the constraints that traditionally have been necessary in our schools.

Modernism/post-modernism

The world in which that type of structure was created, and which that type of structure served and reflected, has gone. In Chapter 3, Fig 3.1, there is a summary of the main differences between the modern world, which is dying, and the post-modern world in which we are now living. In brief, we have moved from a world which was seen to be linear and controllable into a world which is seen to be non-linear and chaotic. The former world was organised on the basis of hierarchies, lines of control, predictability. Instead, now, we are increasingly seeing businesses which have flat or nearly flat management structures. Global companies are run by small groups of people who personify the vision and allow a multitude of small local teams to carry out the work.

Schools, because of societal and governmental pressures and because there is a great inertia in so large a system, still reflect, in the main, the modern world, and are still hierarchical, with most of the structures being still bureaucratic. Schools still organise learning in timed packages, and still organise children in chronological groups, despite knowing that in a class of 11-year-olds doing mathematics there may be a mathematical ability range of seven years (Cockroft, 1982). Society still compels schools to test children when they reach a certain age, rather than when they are ready for the test – a continuing sign of a hierarchy which used and uses the testing procedure to ensure a sufficient number of failures. Imagine the uproar if the government announced that everybody wanting to take the driving test had to do so on the first Friday after reaching their 18th birthday.

Non-linearity

It was a world which believed in linear causality, whereas we now know that B does not necessarily follow A with any degree of certainty. Children's day-to-day experience is non-linear; children themselves and the ways in which they develop are non-linear. Things are, in short, messy, and schools in trying to control events as if everything is plannable and orderable are increasingly asynchronous. We will be looking in greater detail at this aspect of the topic in the next chapter, but for the moment it is enough to stress that in too many schools managers operate on the assumption that cause and effect are discoverable, linear and controllable. They have been protected in this old-fashioned attitude by the demands for school development plans emanating from another power culture – the government.

The central thesis of this book is that the learning of the individual child has been compromised by a range of features, notably the National Curriculum with its emphasis on knowledge and management, on systems and structures, on set times for testing, and on 'value for money', a totally meaningless phrase.

We are not suggesting a conspiracy to deny, but rather a coalition of factors which, when taken together, have led to a drift away from what most teachers claim to be the core purpose of education – the learning of the individual.

We argue that there has been an incremental shift away from individual learning to collective knowledge, from organisations serving individuals to individuals accommodating organisations. This process is not easy to describe because of the gradual nature of the change. Eco (1986), using Wittgenstein's (1953) notion of a game, proposes a model of incremental change.

Games are different activities that display some 'family resemblance', as Wittgenstein put it. Consider the following sequence:

$$\begin{bmatrix} 1 \\ abc \end{bmatrix} \quad \begin{bmatrix} 2 \\ bcd \end{bmatrix} \quad \begin{bmatrix} 3 \\ cde \end{bmatrix} \quad \begin{bmatrix} 4 \\ def \end{bmatrix}$$

Suppose there is a series of political groups in which group 1 is characterised by the features *abc*, group 2 by the features *bcd*, and so on. Group 2 is similar to group 1, since they have two features in common; for the same reason, 3 is similar to 2, and 4 is similar to 3.

Eco points out that although groups 1 and 4 have no common features, because they are in a series there remains an 'illusory transivity' – a family resemblance.

Much of what goes on in school bears only a family resemblance to learning. We say this not because for one moment do we want to join the 'teacher-bashing' brigade. That brigade is motivated by a need to find scapegoats and to exert control, and we feel no such needs. Rather we say this because the pressures exerted by the government on the teaching profession have all been directed towards group acquisition of content, of knowledge, and this emphasis has been caused by two parts of the same ideology. The first part says that all societal problems can be solved by 'market forces'; to 'solve' the problem of education, competition must be introduced, and competition can best be introduced by league tables. Therefore the group results for any school take on paramount importance.

The second part of the ideology says that intelligence is a fixed quantity, and the sooner children are sorted into their proper groupings, the easier it will be to school them into their correct societal slots. Some schools have successfully resisted these pressures, and in them there is an emphasis on individual learning – the pure *abc* definition. However, we also know that in some schools there has been drift, a drift to something like *bcd*. We also know that in some schools the drift has been total, and there is in place an attitude towards learning which is *def*. For this last group of schools and for the children and teachers in them, learning has been redefined in terms of the efficient transmission of knowledge structured according to the dictates of organisational neatness. Yet, because of an 'illusory transivity' it is possible for both those inside and those outside the organisation to believe that children are individually learning.

Learning at the core

To recapture that position we describe as *abc*, the situation in which there is total focus on the individual's learning; we believe that there is a need for a radical reconceptualisation of the education system and of the philosophical substructure. This book will attempt such a reconceptualisation. We will argue that it is possible to reinstate learning, individual learning, as the core activity, and that in fact if we do not, schools as we know them will go deeper and deeper into crisis. As Thomas Kuhn (1962, p 85) argues:

> *The transition from a paradigm in crisis to a new one from which a new tradition of normal science can emerge is far from a cumulative process, one achieved by an articulation or extension of the old paradigm. Rather it is a reconstruction of the field from new fundamentals, a reconstruction that changes some of the field's most elementary theoretical generalisations as well as many of its paradigm methods and applications . . . there will be a decisive difference in the modes of solution.*

This chapter opened with the statement that we need to shift the paradigm, that we have to change our concept of what we mean by 'a school', and we have to change our understanding of all those words that are nested in our current understanding of 'school'.

At the heart of the next century's school will be the clear moral imperative that the individual's learning is paramount. Moreover, there will be the passionate commitment to the knowledge that neither a child nor that child's learning can be neatly compartmentalised for a bureaucracy's ease – the child and the child's learning will be treated holistically. There will be an acknowledgement that no one building called 'a school' can contain the range of resources needed to enable that learning. There will be, in the community, areas in which people learn, but they will scattered around the community and be used by all members in it. There will be an acknowledgement that no one collection of teachers will be sufficient. In the future, and at present in a few innovative institutions, at any one moment, Mrs A is a teacher; at the next she is an ancillary helper; at the next she is a learner. A student can be a learner and a teacher, and both at the same time. Those debilitating dichotomies will be eroded. The neat organisational boxes of subjects and times will be scrapped, because information is ubiquitous, non-time-bounded, and because deep learning cannot be contained by preordained labels. Leadership will be accepted as the possession of the many and not the prerogative of the few. Teams of adults, with teachers in the majority and helped by 'para-teachers', will have as their responsibility the learning of groups of children and their own learning, and they will have the responsibility over the allocation and use of the necessary resources. There will be in each team an intellectual and emotional commitment to the moral imperative, and the headteacher's job will be, in part, to articulate, strengthen and demonstrate that imperative. At the centre of this fluid, learning-centred organisation there will be the clear knowledge, the certainty, that learning is unpredictable, sometimes dangerous, often hilarious and unique to each individual. The organisation will be, therefore, almost undetectable on charts, but vivid in the interplay of people wholly concerned with learning.

Postscript

Stephen Jay Gould, in a 1996 review of *Charles Darwin: Voyaging* by Janet Browne, asks: 'Why Darwin?' He was a genial but feckless student at school, at Edinburgh University where he abandoned his medical studies, and at Cambridge where he spent his time gambling, drinking and hunting. There was nothing in his childhood or youth that gave any indication of the man he was to be.

'I think,' Gould writes, 'that any solution to this key puzzle in Darwinian biography must begin with a proper exegesis of intelligence – one that rejects Charles Spearman's old notion of a single scalar quantity recording overall mental might ... Instead, we need a concept of intelligence as a substantial set of largely independent attributes.' He goes on to cite the work done by Thurstone, Guilford and Gardner (1993) on developing the concept of multi-intelligences, and then states:

> ... the theory of multiplicity includes an important historical and philosophical consequence for understanding human achievement ... if intelligence were a single, innately provided and largely invariant quantity that could be plotted on a single scale, then we might frame a predictive and largely biological model of achievement with a predominant basis in bloodlines and a substrate in neurology ... If the sum of a person's achievement must be sought in a subtle combination of differing attributes, each affected in marvelously varying ways by complexities of external circumstances and the interplay of psyche and society, then no account of particular accomplishment can be drawn simply from prediction based on inherited mental rank.

3

■ ■ ■

Our Children's World

I wrote another book then, The Age of Unreason. *Its central philosophical theme was that change was now, rather obviously, discontinuous; no longer was change a straight projection of past trends into the future. When change is discontinuous, I argued, the success stories of yesterday have little relevance to the problems of tomorrow; they might even be damaging. The world, at every level, has to be reinvented to some extent. Certainty is out; experiment is in.*
(Charles Handy, *Beyond Certainty*)

This chapter will present a sketch map of the world in which the children at present in our schools may, in the near future, be living, working, having their being. That world is going to be very different from the one we are accustomed to; changes will be profound, discontinuous and very rapid. The only certainty our children will have is that there is uncertainty. It is perhaps the sheer speed of change that makes it so difficult for humans to cope. For thousands of years, the rate at which humans travelled, the ways in which they communicated information, the numbers they could kill in any one engagement, altered very little indeed. The rate of travel, for example, was governed by the speed at which we could run, or, later, the speed of the fastest horse, and this maximum speed remained the same for thousands of years. The train accelerated this speed in the last century, the car at the end of that century, and the plane, in effect, right at the beginning of this. Only after the 1939–45 war did we glimpse the possibility of rocket travel, and, if we use the idea of human history being compressed into 24 hours, then space travel at thousands of miles per hour, guided and made possible by the fusion of rocket technology, computers and miniaturisation, has occurred in the last few minutes.

Until the Gutenberg revolution, the oral transmission of information, together with the limited production of manuscripts by religious orders, governed both the speed and the range of the processing of information. Now, the optic fibre carrying thousands of telephone messages, together with interlinked satellites and computers, has stitched the world into a seamless garment of instantaneous communication.

Those two examples, of space travel and real-time communication, point to another variable in any look into the future. Fundamental revolutions, revolutions which change the way we live and therefore the way we perceive the world, occur when two or more technological advances fuse together. The horseshoe and the plough made the agricultural revolution possible; barbed wire and the machine gun changed how we waged war; rocketry and nuclear science gave us the possibility of eliminating life on the planet.

Furthermore, we often totally mistake the uses to which a new piece of technology can be put. When radio first came on the scene, it was thought that its only use would be to aid ship-to-shore communication, and thereby be a great advance in maritime safety. Only after it had been in place for a few years was the possibility of its use for entertainment perceived. Some will argue at present that those millions of homes with PCs in them are using only a small proportion of the power and facilities available; such a criticism is probably true, but it may well be that we have not yet discovered how we will finally use the computing power accessible to us. It may well be, as some computer scientists are saying now, that we will switch from the personal computer to the network computer, a simple, smart box which draws down the power and programs we require when we require them from the Internet. It may well be that the power will not have to be in the home, but centrally held and called upon by the individual to meet a particular need or solve an immediate problem.

Schools and the business of change

Altogether, this list of caveats makes futurology a fraught exercise. Nevertheless, it is essential to attempt it, because there is taking place now a shift in the way our world is organised and the way in which we see reality; therefore, there has to be a parallel paradigm shift in schools in order that they do not become asynchronous with the society that they intend to serve.

The last caveat relates to the wide variation in the degree to which schools have accepted the need to change, and have in fact changed. Some have barely shifted their ways of operating and the assumptions that underpin those ways; some have changed under protest; some have adopted new ways of working in some aspects of their organisations; some have changed in radical ways, both organisationally and, more importantly, in the beliefs and attitudes that inform their day-to-day operations and their planning. The aim of the chapter is to summarise the influences that will impinge on the world our children will inhabit, and then point to how these influences affect schools and what happens in them. The aim is not to convert; rather, there will be a listing of the influences that will impinge on the world our children will inhabit, together with indications as to how these influences may affect schools and what happens in them. It is, of course, the responsibility of the leaders in our schools to decide how they are to react to what is outlined in this chapter.

Post-modernism

Change is discontinuous because it is occurring at so many levels in our lives and in so many different areas at the same time. Change is occurring at an ever-increasing speed and in so many aspects of our lives because it is caused by a concatenation of discoveries, offshoots from those discoveries and unexpected applications of those inventions. Underlying this combination of new technologies, in turn influencing the uses to which they are put and influenced by them, is a fundamental shift in the way we think. This chapter will not even attempt a history of Western thought since the end of the Age of Faith; it is not a guide to current philosophy. There is a need, however, to sketch in what is meant by this shift in philosophical outlook because otherwise it will not be possible to make a coherent attempt at describing the ethical framework within which schools will need to work.

What is occurring at this time might be summed up by saying that we are moving from the 'modern' to the 'post-modern'. The problem with such a neat formula, however, is that it masks as much as it reveals. There have been almost as many meanings attached to the term 'post-modernism' as there have been people using it. This multiplicity of meanings, however, is of itself an indication of what is meant by the term. It is not a rigid philosophy; it does not have a set of rules by which one can discover if one is or is not post-modern; it is not a political club with a set of beliefs to which one subscribes. Rather it is a fluidity of uncertainty, an acceptance of an unmapped territory where you, together with other like-minded people, will create a map, knowing that as you put the finishing touches to it, you will need to change it.

We are living, at present, in a 'modern' world and a 'post-modern' world simultaneously. In part, this duality exists because clear breaks do not occur. We did not stop agriculture when we moved into the industrial age; the degree of importance changed, and the metaphors with which we created our reality changed, but agriculture continued, and has, of course, continued to this day. Similarly, the attitudes and ways of thinking that characterise modernity continue, and will continue. One has only to listen to the cries of those who want to maintain the clear hierarchies and orders of the modern world to realise that the break has not been a clean one. Furthermore, history does not neatly change course on a single day; only with the 20:20 vision of hindsight can we say that such-and-such marked the beginning or the end of an era. To those living at the time, there was no such clarity. When we look back we can say that the acceptance of the earth's roundness was one such turning point. The planet's demotion from being the centre of the universe, the acceptance of Newton's laws, Descartes' 'I think therefore I am' and the change from a predominantly agricultural society to an industrial one are all points after which it was impossible to view the world in the same way as we had before.

The start of the post-modern era – the shift from certainty – might be said to have started with the publication of the *Origin of the Species* by Darwin, and was accelerated by the splitting of the atom and the establishment of quantum physics. In each case, the absolute certainties by which we had lived, the foundations of our reality, were destroyed by a discovery: humans lose their unique place in the chain of life; the atom is not the smallest indivisible unit; the scientist cannot stand outside the box, and the Newtonian laws do not hold sway over all matter.

The major differences between the modern and the post-modern are listed in Fig 3.1. At the end of this chapter there will be an analysis of what these changes might imply for the way we organise our schools. This part of the chapter looks at some of the major aspects of post-modernism, and in particular it will stress the possible impact on the individual.

The shift to personal responsibility

The first point is that the post-modernist world puts very heavy emphasis on personal responsibility. In the past we have been able to look to a variety of hierarchies to give us our sense of values, whether those values relate to music, literature or our slot in society. The canon of great works was established by the dons in the English faculties of the 'top' universities, that canon was studied by undergraduates and by those hoping to be undergraduates, and the idea that there was something called 'great literature' was generally accepted. The fact that many of the books and the writers in the list in one generation were not there in another did not have any impact on the main idea of there being something called 'literature' which was defined by a small group of people at the top of a clear hierarchy (*see* Eagleton, 1983, for further discussion).

Such a simple construction can no longer be accepted as a basis on which to build our sense of values. The argument that the abandonment of deference to hierarchies leads to anarchy or to a general loss of proper aesthetic appreciation is false. At the point of transition, between the acceptance of hierarchies and the exercise of personal responsibility, there may well be confusion; it is arguable that the disaffection visible in sectors of society today are manifestations of that confusion. The problem arises from there being two contrary forces existing side by side: one pushes the individual towards a backward-looking acceptance of handed-down rules and values, and the other pushes the individual towards personal responsibility but without giving the structures and help that are necessary in the early stages. In takes time for the truth to be

Modernism	Post-modernism
Bureaucracy: – slow change – rule bound	Shared, networked, flexible, adapting rapidly to change
Compartmentalisation, fragmentation	Unifying, linking, crossing boundaries
Dualism: – man versus nature – man conquering nature	Wholeness: – humans part of nature – our fates joint and inseparable
Dichotomies: – male–female – objective–subjective – rational–intuitive – scientific–imaginary	Two parts of the same Scientists are in the box, Both ways of encapsulating our truth
Linearity	Non-linearity
Scientifically verifiable truth	Relativism, societal context
Reality 'out there', discoverable	We create our reality
An ultimate knowledge	No such thing
Teaching	Learning together
Belief in progress	No such belief
Certainty	Uncertainty

Fig. 3.1 Comparison of modernism with post-modernism

accepted that an increase in personal responsibility is the most obvious result of the abandonment of deference. Together with others we establish interpretive communities (Fish, 1980), and thereby work to make our own set of judgements within a clear ethical framework. Reliance on a, largely, self-appointed hierarchy no longer is acceptable.

There is, however, a danger in this shift from a hierarchically structured sense of values to a much more personal one in that it can lead to self-centredness, and this in turn can lead to self-indulgence and overweening self-importance.

There are countless examples in the current pop world of such a distortion resulting from a diminution of externally imposed structures. One of the challenges facing schools today is the establishment of a sense of community, an interpretive community, that operates within a framework of ethics and values that is founded on timeless principles to which the individual voluntarily subscribes, but which at the same time enables the individual to learn free of the shackles of hierarchically imposed norms.

The school or factory

If the body of what constitutes essential knowledge cannot be handed to us as a given, one consequence is that there is no one method of transmitting the knowledge that is to be explored and ingested. Since universal education came into being, a factory approach to the organisation of schools has been the general mode. Such an organisation is not surprising, as the state schools were established in order to provide for the children of the workers in the factories. In the factories, work was divided up into the smallest possible units, workers were given no responsibility for the work they carried out, and they were tightly controlled, roughly on a manager-to-managed ratio of ten to one, and the whole enterprise looked to a 'boss' for direction. Schools divided the work of educating the children into small units, and there was a hierarchy to which all looked for direction. In passing, it is worth noting that one of the major difficulties facing those schools in which there are people who want to change is the dependency culture that the hierarchical system engenders.

The analogy with the old-fashioned factory can be extended to the shape and division of the buildings, the rigid adherence to timetables that ignore individual differences, and the compartmentalisation which allows for no holistic view of what the factory/school is trying to achieve.

The analogy with the old-fashioned factory is clear enough, but, as will be discussed later in Chapter 4, such an atomistic system which leaves the learner with little or no responsibility for his or her learning is inadequate to meet the needs of tomorrow's adults.

The school as interpretive community

To return to the idea of interpretive communities. If we do away with, or no longer find useful or appropriate, the structures that our parents and their forefathers found useful, we still need structures within which to live, and thereby create meaning. We create meaning, or our reality, partly on our own and partly through interacting with others. That interaction is an act of interpretation; you and I together interpret our experiences, start to know each other's reality and thereby create a community of two into which we both invest reality and from which we extract a different and larger reality. In other words, interpretive communities establish their own reality.

However, there is another, and vital, ingredient in the establishment of the interpretive community. Over recent years there have been many examples of closed, hermetic communities, cults that have created their own meaning but then have been consumed by acts of the most appalling barbarity. The essential feature that was missing was a reference point outside the community, and outside the community's time. That reference point is the ethical, spiritual principles that have supported and guided human societies for hundreds of years. Those basic spiritual teachings and moral precepts are remarkably similar, regardless of race, religion or time. Any community that loses touch with them is in mortal danger of losing its moral core.

The modernist view was, and is, that there is an ultimate reality 'out there' which, by dint of the right questioning and investigation we will all come to understand. The post-modernist does not find such a view acceptable. There is no such reality. We build our world, our reality, through discourse. Within the interpretive community over a period of time, we explore our feelings, ideas, reactions to events, our relationships. We establish a shared vocabulary and understanding through a process which is dynamic. Such a community is no easy option. Critics of post-modernism frequently imply that there is something intellectually lazy about not sticking to the handed-down 'truths' of the modern world. However, battling to create meaning, knowing that we are our language, exploring our history that has given us that language and the contemporary setting that is currently shaping who and what we are is not easy. However, such discourse is one of the essential differences between the post-modern and the modern. The modern stresses that there is a set block of knowledge that is external to ourselves and has to be ingested by us if we are to be full members of society. The post-modern says that knowledge is relational, is contingent upon the people within the discourse, and is vital and changing.

Created versus mandated knowledge

It is this difference that forms the topic of the fundamental debate between the two ways of looking at the world, and it is the debate which goes to the heart of how schools see themselves. If knowledge is viewed as an external body of information, and the content of that body is decided on by people in a hierarchy and not by the teachers, then schools are merely passive conduits. If, however, knowledge is seen to be that which emerges from the interaction between the information of the disciplines on the one hand and the understanding and experience of the individual on the other – in other words knowledge is seen to be something that is created, not imparted – then schools take on a totally different character. Currently, it is the modernist hierarchy's view that holds sway. The third section of this chapter will deal with some of the ways by which schools can begin to wrench the argument away and start to establish their own grounds for debate. There will, however, be a tenacious hold by the hierarchy to the argument that there must be a body of knowledge for schools to impart.

This argument is false, but there is a superficial credibility. One of the acknowledged problems in schools before the establishment of the National Curriculum was the arbitrary nature of the curriculum that some of our children experienced. The curriculum was unsatisfactory because, although schools adhered to the notion that they had to impart items of knowledge, many schools demonstrated a quite arbitrary method of deciding why some items were to be included and some not. The problem has not, of course, been solved by the National Curriculum. Again, there is no explicit or implicit rationale which underpins the collection of items that are included, but by imposing the NC through an Act of Parliament, there is a patina of respectability, and of course central control, over the arbitrary collection of subjects that is included.

It is worth remembering that before the NC was imposed there was an interpretive community – LEA officers, teachers, HMI – that over a period of time, through discourse, had come to an agreement over the areas of study that all children should experience, but left the day-to-day content to schools. The resulting curriculum was a very solid outcome for that community, and was a rebuttal of the idea that only through central control can we avoid chaos.

Dichotomies and control

The tendency to an 'either/or' argument, in this case either the National Curriculum or chaos, is one of the chief marks of the modernist view of how the world works. One of the aims of our schools must be the reduction, and if possible the elimination, of these imposed dichotomies of the Enlightenment. One of the strongest currents in post-modernism is seeing things holistically, seeing objects as points on spectra which demonstrate linkage rather than as opposites, mutually exclusive, separate. In large part, the dichotomy is a tool which enables hierarchies to control, and control is a strong feature of the modernist world. Let us take as an example the refusal over many years to give women the vote. The easiest way to counter the argument which says that women must have the vote as it is natural justice, and that men and women, being equal, must be treated equally, is to apply a dichotomy – men and women are entirely different. Men are leaders; women are subservient. Subservient people cannot have the vote. The discussion stops there and political control remains in male hands, or at least it did until that world view was shattered.

Such a desire for control runs deep. There was a deeply held belief that over time, and through the application of the scientific method, humans could achieve control over their lives and over the rest of nature. We are beginning to realise the cost of such a notion. The simple-minded polarisation of the world into warring opposites, possible through the creation of dichotomies, has skewed our perception for many years. We need to emphasise ways of seeing holistically.

Through dichotomies one stopped an argument. There were no shades of meaning, no fine gradations of change; the object was either rational or irrational, objective or subjective. Through dichotomising the world, one can achieve closure, and by closure one stops discussion or argument, and this stoppage gives further control. If, in an argument about who does what in the house, I state that such-and-such is 'woman's work', I close the discussion – or at least I did until such mandated closure was no longer accepted by the partner in the discussion. The modernist world view is posited, in large measure, on a long list of such opposites – man vs woman; man (sic) vs nature; control vs anarchy; black vs white. Such opposites gave a sense of certainty, of order, and, above all, of control.

Whose reality?

A hierarchy's control, furthermore, fixes what is accepted as reality. For example, a school decides that this class of children will learn English between 9:30 and 10:05. The first bizarre notion is that anyone can really think that he or she can mandate what someone else will learn. In the second place, the reality for four children in that class is that they cannot learn English, or anything else, at that time. They come to school not having had any breakfast, and they are entirely unable to pay attention. As their reality is in conflict with the headteacher's reality, and the headteacher is in a hierarchical relation above them, their reality is denied. It is 'their fault' that they are not learning, and the English, and other lessons, continue for those four regardless of *their* reality. The headteacher has a view of a superordinate reality which runs something like this: schools are organised like this; children fit in with that organisation; any child that does not fit in is disruptive; the ultimate reality of school organisation cannot accept any infringement.

The modernist, looking always for a validation that is 'out there', over and above the individual or even a group of individuals, denies that new experiences, one's own or other people's, can alter an immutable reality or can lead to new meanings. Such new meanings would, of course, expose one to uncertainty. It was certainty that was so much sought by the modernist world, and it is certainty that has proved a chimera to the post-modern world.

Identity

The establishment of opposites was also a search for domination and identity. If I could point to something which I proclaimed was my opposite, I established 'the other' and thereby gave myself the authority to control, govern, brutalise or feel, ironically, inferior to that other. Furthermore, by the identification of 'the other', I established and then reinforced my own identity. It might be said that, for example, the modern man shaped his sense of identity as much by *not* being what he thought of as a woman as by having any clear idea of what being a man in fact meant. Similarly, by believing that 'nature' was something other than the human race, that the human race was set over and intended to be in control of nature, the exploitation of nature was not merely possible but actually lauded. The post-modernist view is that, in part or as a whole, we are that other; that humans and nature, for example, are the same, and that in the conflict between them there lies the destruction of both.

The scientific method

Two further shifts are taking place, two strands which are closely interrelated. One of the major beliefs of the modern world was in the 'scientific method'. In very brief, and possibly over-simple, terms, belief in the scientific method gave humans the certainty that progress to an earthly Utopia was possible; disease could be controlled, death postponed, economic prosperity available to everyone. Science would provide. Further, by the application of the scientific method, solutions could be found to any problem. By breaking down any object into its component parts, we could discover its workings; the whole was no more and no less than the sum of the parts, and by knowing the parts we would know the whole. The scientist, standing outside the box, objective and impartial, carefully dissecting whatever was the target for investigation and demonstrating how it worked, was to be the creator of that Utopia.

We now know that the scientist is inside the box; that the questions that he or she asks are culturally and historically bound and influence the answers; that there is no such thing as objectivity (see Barone (1992) on subjectivity, Eisner (1992) on objectivity and Guba (1992) on relativism); that the whole is far greater than the sum of the parts; that 'progress', however defined, is not cost-free. Belief that it is possible to have rational control over our own lives, let alone over others', is no longer possible, and total knowledge of any topic is equally impossible. We are beginning to see the arrogance in the idea of man (sic) lording (sic) it over nature, controlling nature, exploiting nature. The neat dichotomies of the modern world which gave us a mythology of ultimate power and orderliness have gone, and the partitions which that order brought are beginning to crumble (see Usher and Edwards, 1994, for further discussion).

Perhaps the best symbol of the post-modernist view of the world is that photograph of the world taken, a few years ago, by an astronaut. The world, blue, green and white, hangs totally alone in blue space; no sign of humans can be seen, just the wholeness of a living unit. That photograph, more than any number of books and speeches, gave to many the feeling of the fragility of our planet, and of the oneness of life on it.

The world around us

This chapter will later tease out some of the implications for schools in a post-modernist world, but before doing so it is necessary to sketch in some further trends that are changing the world that our young people will live in in the twenty-first century. This is not new ground. There has been a plethora of articles and books about what the next century might look like. This part of the chapter will note some of the the main trends, and later try to estimate in what ways schools might reasonably react. There is a degree of artificiality, imposed by the linearity of a book, in dividing the section on post-modernism from this section, because post-modernism affects in a multitude of ways how the world is changing, and how the world is changing alters and re-emphasises aspects of post-modernism. To add to the complexity, some items mentioned in this section interact with each other and may produce unexpected results and outcomes. An additional complication is that, although the 'we' in this section refers to the developed world, in fact countries within that world are at a number of different points in their development, and countries which have hitherto been seen to be part of the 'developing world' are catching up with or even overtaking some of the countries in the developed world. The linear book is not the best means to describe a non-linear world.

We have moved from extracting our wealth from industry and manufacturing to a world in which information and the knowledge of how to use it are the wealth-creators. Nations that have the capacity to add value by adding 'smartness' to a product are the nations that are wealthy. By 'smartness' is meant additional information being built into the product. A telephone that merely enables you to listen and talk to someone is no longer enough; it must be able to give a message when you are not there and take a message; it should double as a fax; it could be plugged into a cable and a television set to give access to 24-hour shopping. By combining technologies and information, consumer goods become more and more sophisticated and, at the same time, bring wealth to those that create them.

We are also moving from a world of relative stability into a world of fluid alliances and endless possibilities, some benign, some malign. During the Cold War there was a certain dependability in the lines of antagonism that were fixed, and from the aptly named policy of MAD (Mutually Assured Destruction) we could draw, perversely enough, a degree of comfort. Now, with the breakup of the Soviet Union and the recrudescence of nationalism, wars and the rumours of wars surround us. The unpredictability of such a world is enormously more dangerous because, on top of the enormous stocks of conventional weapons that we have created and continue to create, there is the nuclear legacy left to possible use by unstable individuals.

The world of work and non-work

We are beginning to see new patterns of work emerging, and the new patterns of non-work. If we look to the United States we can see these patterns very clearly. It is in the demography of work that we can see the most obvious changes. Fewer and fewer people are working in manufacturing; one estimate is that by 2000 only some 10 per cent of those in work will be working in manufacturing. A decade ago, the top 500 companies in the USA employed 20 million people. Today it is fewer than 10 million. More and more will be working in service industries and in those sectors in the economy which deal in 'brain work' – lawyers, electronic engineers, architects, doctors. Work increasingly goes to where labour is cheapest, and one of the themes that emerged in the Presidential election of 1996 was a suggestion that what was needed was a return to strict protectionism to stop work fleeing from the high-cost factories in the US. However, what is less obvious, but is much more influential in the long run, are the underlying trends in the social aspects of the economy (*see* Head, 1996). In very broad terms, the rich are getting richer and there are fewer of them, and the poor are getting poorer and there are more of them. The average pay of rank-and-file workers in the US has fallen, in real terms, by 18 per cent between 1973 and 1995. Between 1979 and 1989, by contrast, the salaries of executives increased in real terms by 19 per cent, or, if the changes in the taxation levels are taken into account, by 66 per cent. In the United Kingdom we are seeing very similar trends. Five per cent of the population controls 51 per cent of the nation's wealth.

What we are also seeing for the first time in industrialised countries is that the arrival of an economic upturn, or the rise in overall productivity, brings no real increase in the number of people employed. Head (1996) quotes McKinsey's study (1993) which found that when Japanese corporations achieved higher rates of productivity, not only was there no increase in the number of people employed but there was an actual decline. Productivity is increased, in successful countries, by smarter means of production, not by hiring more people. Such a finding should not come as a surprise; we have only to look at British agriculture in the last century to see how productivity has increased beyond all expectations, but now less than 5 per cent of the population works on the land.

Head (1996) also found, contrary to the statements by our politicians, that the educational and vocational qualifications of the workforce were of very little importance. When he spoke to the personnel managers of two major Japanese firms in the UK, they both said that qualities such as the ability to work in teams, dexterity and enthusiasm were the qualities looked for. He suggests that one of the reasons German industry is going through difficulties is that their tradition of the highly trained and educated *Meister* and *Techniker* is actually holding back the improvements in the methods of production that have been achieved by the Japanese. The term that is used to describe new production methods is 'lean' production. It is lean production that gives the maximum value-added, and lean production does not require large numbers of highly or even well paid, skilled workers. Lean production depends on making the production process as simple as possible, and using computers and robots to the maximum. The disturbances in early 1997 in South Korea arose, in part, from the realisation of the government and business leaders that the job-for-life, inflexible practices of the past are now holding back that economy's continued rise.

The changes in production methods not only affect blue-collar workers; it is increasingly affecting white-collar workers, middle managers and clerical workers. Much of the work traditionally carried out by a clerk and a middle manager can increasingly be done by a computer with the right software. Head (1996) refers to Hammer and Champney's findings in, for instance, IBM, in which the productivity of the credit section increased by 10,000 per cent following 're-engineering'. (Although Hammer and Champney's (1993) book was aimed specifically at industry and commerce, nevertheless some of the basic messages apply very clearly to the world of education.) Head (1996) lists the very many companies in Hammer and Champney's book that have analysed their core activity, and then created the computer hardware and software to do that work at speeds and with levels of efficiency undreamt of in the days of clerks and middle managers. The downside of those changes has, obviously, been a vastly increased unemployment rate among those workers.

The point cannot be over-stressed. What we are seeing in firms that have previously been the bastions of the middle-class career is an increase in the amount of computer power being used, a reduction in the number of people being employed, and a decrease in the educational levels needed for those that are employed. For example, the human resources manager of one of the firms that has gone into the area of 24-hour banking by phone said recently that what he was looking for in new employees was not the traditional two or three A levels that used to be the passport to a banking career, but rather a pleasant telephone voice, and the ability to project care and personality over the phone; the answers to the questions raised by the customers were contained in the expert system that was in the software at the young person's fingertips. As an American executive told Head (Head, 1996), it takes only two months to train workers in basic computer skills; it took very much longer to train a young person to become a banker.

A further feature of the work scene that our children will be facing is highlighted by the term 'contingent workforce'. The pattern of work that obtained until comparatively recently was of a person leaving school or university and working 48 hours a week for 48 weeks in the year for about 40 years. That work could very well have been in the same firm, and if not in the same firm, then in the same area of employment – so a teacher would move from school to school to gain promotion or for other reasons, but the expectation was that education would remain the field of employment. That pattern is decreasingly the one that obtains now and in the future. Charles

Handy in his book *The Empty Raincoat* (1994), and in particular in the chapter entitled 'Spliced Lives', deals with the new patterns of our lives in detail. In brief, for those of us who work, we may well compress the 100,000 hours traditionally worked in a lifetime into 30 years. We will build up a portfolio of experiences culled from a number of different firms and in different disciplines. In between working periods there will, there must, be periods of intensive education, because the methods of doing a particular job will be changing all the time, or because the job to be done is one that was not even in existence a few years previously. One CEO recently said that if you are doing the same thing in the same way in five years' time, then you are in the wrong.

We will work in teams that change according to the demands of the task. We will work for fees, for a job done, rather than for time completed. We will take increasing responsibility for our own health care and pensions. There will be salaried people employed by a particular company for a long period of time, but those people will be in a very small minority. It is worth noting at this point that the largest employer in the USA is Manpower Inc, a staffing agency.

The consequences of this new economy, this 'ruthless' economy as Head (1996) calls it, is an increase in poverty. In a recent book on the American poor (Davis, 1996), the author estimates that there are some 60 million poor in the US – the richest economy in the world; 26 million of them, half of them children, are dependent on soup kitchens, and between 12 and 15 million of them are 'persistently, intractably, Underclass poor'. It is the emergence of an underclass, deemed by some observers as being unemployable, that is another, growing, feature in the world we inhabit. This underclass is not merely poor in economic terms, but it is also 'information poor'. It cannot access and use the information that is available, and this increases their vulnerability and lack of hope of obtaining a job. Not having a job decreases their chance of accessing the information. It is a classic vicious circle.

The signs of this poverty are all too easy to detail and see. The problem is exacerbated in that at the same time as the economy is 'downsizing' and making more people unemployed, so governments are increasingly looking to ways to decrease the state's involvement in welfare and long-term aid programmes. The number of beggars on the streets of Los Angeles who were recently well paid workers in Silicone Valley; the lack of public hospitals in central Detroit; the headline in a recent edition of *The Observer* – 'Now it's the DIY welfare state' (1996) – these and very many similar indicators are all signs of the dramatic changes in the expectations that our children can reasonably have of the world in which they are going to live their adult lives.

Mega-trends

Apart from these major trends in the world of work, there are other aspects of life in the twenty-first century that need to be mentioned. There is a growing split between the centre and the periphery visible in this country and in some others in which a right-wing government is in power. The easiest label for it is 'polarisation' – there is the paradox of the centre taking more and more powers, but making the individual units at the periphery more and more accountable to their clients and customers. The education service is a clear example. Since 1988, the centre has accrued a vast panoply of powers, and the degree of control hitherto wielded by local education authorities has sharply declined. At the same time, through the publication of inspection reports, the devolution of almost all, and in the case of grant-maintained schools all, the budget to the individual school, the publication of league tables, the (at least in theory) ability of parents to choose to which school their children are to go – all these have made schools open to public questioning as never before.

Running through the earlier part of the chapter is the theme of the power of the computer, the ubiquitous infiltration of IT. As wealth is a function of the control and use of information, so the reliance upon IT has increased. The effects are numerous, from the vanishing of swathes of jobs, through the change to the idea of lean production, to the virtual organisation. This last means that it is no longer necessary to go to an office to do office work, to a bank to do banking, to go to a university to be a university student. The linking of computer, phone and satellite means that I can get the information that I need, and transmit the information that I need to share, at any time, from any place that has a power supply, and at any time that suits me. It is perhaps this change in the availability of information, and the positioning of the user at the centre, controlling information rather than being controlled by it, that may well have the greatest impact on what schools do and how they do it.

It is also this ease of transfer of information that has created the global economy, making the transfer of vast amounts of money possible throughout the 24-hour day, and at the same time making it possible to switch work to wherever it is most convenient and best priced. US firms use young computer graduates in Bangalore to create their software; the Benefits Agency in the North East of England received its most competitive tender for its work from Taiwan; a major US insurance company has the majority of its claims processed in Cork; the new Mini that is planned will start its design in a company located in England owned by Germans; the engine will be made in Portugal and Brazil, and the latter plant will be part-owned by Chrysler, an American firm. The examples are legion, and they add up to the simple, but profound, message that there is nothing sacrosanct about a national economy, a national firm. They point to the basic fact that it is information that is the commodity which creates wealth.

We are seeing the steady shift of power away from Europe and the eastern seaboard of the United States to the countries of the Pacific rim. The young 'tigers' such as Hong Kong, Singapore, Taiwan and South Korea are investing heavily in education and expanding their economies at a rate which leaves us lagging far behind – Thailand, for example, doubled its GNP in the last ten years. Increasingly these countries are not competing just on low wages, but are competing with value-added goods; for example, Malaysia and South Korea have both become substantial exporters of cars. Singapore will have soon a per-capita wealth exceeding that of the UK.

We are also seeing a sharp move away from the monolithic to the networked company. Toyota, for example, is now nearly equal to General Motors in market share, but has at its core fewer than 1000 people. Beneath those 1000, there is a network of thousands of wholly owned, partly owned and wholly independent companies. Toyota has a structure which is extremely flexible and gives it a huge competitive advantage. It is a perfect example of a major trend away from hierarchies and bureaucracies, because those systems of working have been found to be slow to change, cumbersome, expensive and unable to relate to the needs of the customer, which is the only *raison d'être* for a firm. It is also an example of the ruthless way in which international companies survive; if there is a downturn in demand for Toyota cars, for example, and therefore of their production, many of those small companies will collapse as their only *raison d'être* is to supply Toyota.

The rest of this book could be devoted to outlining some of the facts and figures that our young people are going to be left to cope with. There are two sets to consider: one set relates to excessive population expansion, depletion of the rain forests, the reduction of the number of species, the increase in pollution; the other set suggests that the human race can, through its ingenuity and technology, survive pretty well. Depending on which groupings of these numbers one believes in, one can become either deeply despairing, or mildly optimistic. The pessimists argue that the human race is determined to obliterate itself; the optimists argue that there is no reason to suppose that the capability to adapt and improve that has been a feature of the human race so far is suddenly going to vanish. Such arguments are outside the scope of this book, although they are vital to the discussion of the bases of the philosophy that underpins a school's organisation and methodologies.

Instead, the remainder of this chapter will extract some ideas from what can be seen in the world generally for schools to consider, and see how far adaptations can be made by schools to enable them to face the twenty-first century with a degree of confidence that they are meeting their children's needs and aspirations. We need at this point to declare our hand. It is our belief that schools in the main are entering the twenty-first century with structures and, more importantly, underlying assumptions which are nineteenth century in their origins, or relate to the world of the 1950s and 1960s. There is a great variety in how schools are run, but by the end of the chapter it might be interesting for readers to position their schools in terms of readiness to cope with the next century.

Implications for schools

This chapter has made an arbitrary division between an approach to a philosophy – post-modernism – and a look at some of the trends in work and demography. The division is an attempt to help the reader but there is no such neat division in the way the world operates and changes. For example, the sharp decline in hierarchical ways of organising companies has occurred in part because people's faith in the efficacy of hierarchies has evaporated; but at the same time, our actual ability to eliminate them has come about because, through networked computers, we find that we do not need those information processors and controllers that were middle managers. Philosophy and technical ability are hard to separate. Another example might be in the field of medicine where the belief that a single-minded concentration on the symptoms of the disease (the whole is no more than the sum of its parts) is giving way to the idea that treating the whole person is essential if the person, not just the disease, is to be cured. At the same time, we are increasingly able to see how stress, for instance, manifests itself in ways that are not susceptible to single-point medicine, and we have developed a range of alternative approaches which extend the range of possible responses to a person's illness. Philosophy and the ways we deal with our world are not dichotomous. In what follows, the two threads of the underlying philosophy and the means of putting that philosophy into action will be treated together.

The paradoxes facing schools

Quite obviously, schools are facing a number of paradoxes and challenges. One paradox, discussed below, is that in a society which is changing rapidly, schools are being told that to prosper and for their pupils to prosper they must go 'back to basics', back to a mythical world when all was well with the education system. Another paradox is that schools see the need to expand what they do and how they do it at a time when they are being told by many governments in the developed world that they will have few if any extra resources – 'more for less' is a widely heard cry.

The main challenge is that there is an urgent need for schools to reconsider the basic philosophy by which they operate, and, of course, many have already done so, or are in the process of doing so. The change is, as has been implied, from the certainty that there is a body of knowledge that must be imparted to the children; that there is a fixed and limited intelligence that is predetermined for each child; that intelligence is expressed through one, narrow, set of activities; that head is superior to hand and heart. Such a philosophy predicts the type of organisation that a school has in place, and it is, to put it briefly, an organisation that is geared to enabling teachers to teach, and is not based on the multiple ways in which children learn.

There needs to be a change to a philosophy which believes that there is no limit to the extent to which a child's mind can be expanded; that the only true learning is that which enables the individual to change; that knowledge is created out of the interaction between the individual and the discipline; that there is no set of 'subjects' that must be kept separate, but that there is holistic knowledge, a Gestalt that we need to enable children to see; that the child's needs as a learner predominate. It is also a philosophy which is a lot less safe than we have been accustomed to because learning is unpredictable and unlimitable; we can never be sure where it is going to lead, and we can never set neat, and comfortable, boundaries as to what is to be learnt, nor to the ways in which the learning can be expressed. Learning is spontaneous, unpredictable, fun, passionate, dangerous. Learning is the polar opposite of what modernist, central controllers want or can cope with. Schools based on an ardent belief in having learning at the centre need to be resilient and very adaptable.

The organisation that arises from such a philosophy is far looser than we have seen traditionally: one in which there are truly cooperative classrooms; one in which the adults are themselves learners, very aware of the varieties of ways in which they learn and are therefore always looking for new ways to enable individual children to learn. It is an organisation based on the authority of expertise, rather than the authority of position and office; and as expertise is to be found in all sorts of people, leadership will be dispersed and fluid. It is, above all else, an organisation centred on children and adults as learners. Some schools are already adopting such an organisation, putting at the heart 'managers of learning' who are responsible in the fullest sense for a small group of children, ensuring that the school, as far as resources and human ingenuity allow, adapts to, encourages and satisfies the child's learning needs.

What is our meaning?

Before any change can take place, the school has to examine its current philosophy, and one of the first steps in this examination is to scrutinise the vocabulary it uses. (We explore this topic in more detail in Chapter 8). Everyone in the school has to rediscover the meaning of the central words that the school uses to describe itself to itself and to others, and scrutinise all the para-linguistic signs that it sends out. What do we mean by 'education', 'learning', 'responsibility', 'authority'? How do we celebrate what sorts of activities? How do we reward individuals and groups who surprise us by the excellence of their achievements? What do the signs and forms and letters and notices tell us and outsiders about how we think and what we value? What does our vocabulary tell us about how we view the game that we are playing? By exploring these types of question, and through the slow and steady establishment of meaning, followed by the enquiry into whether what is done in the school is what the school means and wants to be done, only then can a school begin to establish itself as an interpretive community.

Until a school has established itself as an interpretive community, and has done so by a thorough exploration of the words and signs that are its mainstays, it has to accept the meanings that are imposed by those who are in central control. The paradox is that those in central control of education do not explore the words of education in educational terms; they impose a market economy and a modernist control interpretation on them. One has only to listen to the bizarre public comments recently by politicians and others in central control about 'discipline', discussions in which the words 'discipline', 'control', 'order' and 'corporal punishment/the cane' were used almost interchangeably. Schools need to wrench the discourse back from the centre.

The myths of education

Furthermore, those in control of the education system hamper and frustrate those many schools that are trying to change. The control is obvious in such ways as the imposition of the National Curriculum, the assessment system, the overall amount of money that is allocated to the system. The more subtle control is through the mythology that is pervasive, and emanates from the centre but is also echoed by many parents and employers. The myth is that at some time in the past, though the actual time is never specified, education reached a plateau of very near perfection. From that time there has been a steady decline, and now society and education in particular must do all that is possible to return to that time in order to have an education system in which we can all trust and which will do for the nation what an education system is supposed to do. Before dealing with that myth, it is interesting to note a parallel with the argument put forward, often by the same people, that the English language at some time in the past, and again this time is never specified, was perfect and has been in decline ever since, and there is a need urgently to go back to recapture its true essence.

Both these myths are wrong, and wrong for a number of reasons, but here the concern is only with the education myth. First, and most obviously, there was never a time when schools were perfect, or even nearly perfect. Employers have always complained that schools were not producing workers with the right qualifications or skills; parents have always complained that schools were too strict or too relaxed, and in any case were not teaching the children as they had been taught. If we go back to the days of National Service, we can read of the Army Education Corps' enormous problems with actual or functional illiteracy among so many of the conscripts. Go back further, and we have the majority of children leaving school at 12 or 13, with no discernible qualifications. Go back further, and there are Egyptian hieroglyphs complaining of the lack of good order and learning among the young.

Second, the myth is wrong because it suggests that control, strictness, sitting in rows and large doses of rote learning are the ways to re-establish this perfect system of education. It is, of course, the sort of picture one would expect from a modernist bureaucracy: control is of the essence; the bureaucrats' belief is that intelligence is finite and predetermined, and therefore schools must be places into which pupils are made to fit, rather than places which enable pupils to grow.

Third, the myth is wrong because even if there were a time when schools were perfect, to make the leap and say that therefore we should have those sorts of schools again now is totally illogical. Let us pretend for the moment that we can locate this educational Utopia in, say, the early 1950s. Schools at that time, so runs the myth, educated the children to fit in with the mores of those times, produced young people able to take their part in the adult world and in employment, and were places of calm, obedience and deference. Even to start to spell out such a notion shows its simple-minded nature. However, for a little longer we will play this game of make-believe. We take the systems, the range of pedagogies, the styles of relationships, the types and quantities of resources including information in the form of books and, peripherally, the radio, and plonk them down in the schools and the world of 1997. The world is not the same. The idea is nonsensical. The past is not available to us; we cannot pick up from the past those bits that we think we like and force them into the present to solve future questions. The myth is a peculiarly vacuous one, but, unfortunately, a seductive one.

The system and the reluctance to change

A further problem facing the many schools that are changing and want to change is the deeply conservative nature of many parents, employers and politicians when it comes to the matter of education. It is this conservative nature that explains the ready market in which the myth discussed above obtains. Offer the average parent a car with the mechanical qualities and safety features of one made in the middle 1930s, and you would be scorned. Offer a politician suffering a serious illness a hospital equipped on 1940s standards and a team of surgeons who relied on 'good, sound common sense' and ignored 'left-wing, progressive theoretical research' and the politician will reject your offer. However, offer a school run on 'good, old-fashioned lines', with 'traditional discipline and styles of teaching' and the school will be oversubscribed. To be fair, no parent – and indeed no teacher – is prepared to experiment with their children, and there is the feeling that were schools to change the ways in which they have been run for years, there would be a risk of trying out newfangled ideas which might cause harm. It is better, so the argument runs, to stick to 'tried and tested' ways. It is ironic that such an argument is posed only when a school suggests changing to a system that focuses on the child's learning. The introduction of the NC, the imposition of testing at certain arbitrary ages, the change in what is to be examined at 16+, all these innovations came from the centre and were not 'experiments'; they were, the political leaders said, commonsense and necessary ways of improving the system. Again, the discourse has been hijacked from the teachers and needs to be grabbed back.

Another problem is that of funds. 'More for less' is a demand that can be heard in many parts of the world, and from all shades of political parties. The funds properly to equip schools with the technologies they require are not there. Schools have been built with one sort of education in mind, one requiring a plethora of inflexible boxes linked by corridors. There is precious little capital funding available which would enable schools to carry out the necessary alterations to enable them to put in place the range of technologies which pupils need if they are to be properly educated for the world of the twenty-first century. There is no money to repair glaring deficiencies, let alone restructure buildings so that they have the flexibility needed to meet present and future demands.

Finally, numbers of teachers ask that there be no more change for a while. They are suffering, so they claim, from an excess of change, and suggest that they be given time for all the upheavals of the last few years to bed down and become routine. There is, of course, no such option. In a world of stability, or at least of gradual and predictable change, it might have been possible for an institution to remain static and survive. In this world of ever-increasing quantitative change, and change occurring at increasing speed, schools have a stark choice. They can either change, adapting themselves to the new demands and expectations of their students, or they do not change, and therefore decline in credibility, usefulness and relevance. To stand still is to become anachronistic; to be an anachronism is to be of no value to our children.

Despite all these difficulties and problems, there is mounting evidence that schools in very many parts of the English-speaking world are beginning to undertake very radical change. Increasingly teachers and researchers alike are seeing that the old nostra are insufficient. 'Back to basics' is a peculiarly inept rallying cry for those trying to enable young people to live in the twenty-first century. There is a clearly discernible shift away from a concentration on techniques and organisational improvements relating to teaching, towards a focus on learning, and on how cultures and structures can be changed to enable extended and deep learning to take place.

Once again, philosophy and technology merge, the first informing the second, and the second making the first possible to reify. We now know that people have multiple intelligences. We know that children and adults learn in many different ways. A recent piece of research into children being educated at home stated that there are at least 32 different ways in which people learn and the researchers were convinced that that figure was not final. We know that people learn different things at different speeds. However, if we had to rely on the limited resources of the class textbook and the school library, if we had to rely solely on the finite number of teachers that a school can employ on a ratio determined by finance and not pupil need, if we had to rely on the geographical limitations of the school, then we could not answer that diversity of learning needs and types. The arrival of IT has changed, fundamentally, the ways in which we can answer children's needs, and, in turn, has given us new insights into the ways children learn.

Digitalisation means choice

In very brief terms, and to state the obvious, IT has loosened us from the limitations of time and space. In the same way as one can carry out one's banking needs, for example, at any time of the day or night, so one can tap into any information source at will. In the same way as one can discuss a project with colleagues in three countries, have the design completed by a co-worker in a fourth, and the prototype constructed in a fifth all without anyone moving from wherever she or he finds it easiest to work, so one can get a first-rate lecture from a university in another country, a one-to-one tutorial with a tutor a hundred miles away, read a report from a researcher in another continent in real time, and download one's paper to yet another tutor living on the other side of Atlantic. The school is no longer the main place to go to for information. It may well be the place to go to for encouragement, guidance, coaching, socialisation, fun, sport, theatre and a whole slew of community activities, but the prime task of imparting, checking and testing the retention of information need no longer be a main activity to be carried out in a school as we know it today.

School organisations

What sort of organisation does a school require to cope with the sort of flexibility that IT could bring to the world of education? Obviously there is not a single, simple answer. By its very nature, the new world of information and the resultant freedom from old restrictions could not possibly bring in its train the imposition of a single approach. Each school will have certain essentials it must adhere to – the number of days' attendance, and for safety reasons there will be a specified ratio of adults to children. However, the adults need not necessarily be qualified teachers, and teachers will not be teaching the set hours they do now. The boundaries between the school and the community will be permeable to the point at which they become invisible. The terms 'learner' and 'teacher' will become interchangeable according to the time of day and the activity. Schools will become increasingly less self-reliant; they will stop trying vainly to meet the multitudinous needs and expectations of its clients within the strict limitations of its human and material resources. Through local and international networks they will be, and indeed some already are, able to call on people and ideas and approaches to a topic from anywhere in the world, and will be able to contribute their own high-spots of expertise to the network.

The organisation of the institution will be 'loose-tight'; that is, there will be few if any of the lines of management that we know at present. There will be none of the adherence to 35-minute periods, 08:45 start and 15:55 finish. There will, however, be a tight ethical binding, a clear adherence to a community enterprise illumined by a clear vision. There will be, as there is at present in our best schools, a dedication to high achievement in whatever field of ethical human enterprise a child or group of children chooses, a dedication to maximising each person's learning. In such a community, there can be no organisational pattern imposed from without. In the opening chapter of this book, we have attempted to visualise a 'day in the life of' such a community. At present, it is sufficient to say that once schools are given the means and the freedom to respond to the vision of the twenty-first century, they will look and behave very differently from the ways in which they are constrained to behave at present.

4

■ ■ ■

Understanding Learning

The curriculum is to be thought of in terms of activity and experience
rather than of knowledge to be acquired and facts to be stored.
(Haddow Report, 1931)

In Chapter 3, the argument was that the world is chaotic, complex and changing at an exponential rate. At the same time the education system displays every sign of clinging to ways of operating which are at best antiquated and at worst actually dysfunctional. It is surely bizarre that in a post-industrial, multicultural society, the agricultural patterns of the eighteenth century still determine the balance of the school year. The deference to an antiquated mode of production as a determinant of educational processes is, in fact, a highly significant symbol of the problems with our understanding of learning. The core technology of schools still involves teachers teaching, pupils replicating knowledge and being assessed on the extent to which they can retrieve it from memory. What is often missing in the process of schooling is an explicit, systematic and consistent understanding of the ways in which knowledge and skills are received – the emphasis is on transmission.

What is knowledge?

Indeed, a lack of clarity as to what 'knowledge' is underlies many of the cross-currents visible in the education system. Some look on knowledge as being made up of a very large number of items of information stored in a warehouse. Indeed, it would seem clear that such a view is held by those in power, politicians and the various curricular and inspection quangos. What follows, therefore, is in no way intended to be an attack on teachers, but rather an attempt to clarify the two, opposing, meanings that surround the word 'knowledge'. Many would say that the teacher's role is to go to the warehouse, select those items that he or she thinks the class needs or that the state mandates that the children will receive, and then to 'deliver' these items to the class whose responsibility is to memorise them and demonstrate this memorisation later by regurgitating the items on demand. Knowledge, in this view, is fixed, exists in its own right and the decisions as to which items are to be passed on to which pupils and at which time are in the hands of some authority usually situated outside the classroom. This view is essentially hierarchical, and stems from a time when the power structure saw that information equalled power and so information was rationed according to status. The cliché 'deliver', when applied to the curriculum, is a sign of this view. Furthermore, this definition of knowledge is a remnant of those days when pupils could be told that such-and-such a grouping of items of information were what they would need in this or that walk of life. Not so long ago, a person could obtain a job and keep it for an entire working life with a group of five or six 'O' levels being the only academic qualification. Now, the half-life of the value of six GCSEs at Grades A to C reduces rapidly each year.

Knowledge is created

The other meaning of knowledge has at its core the idea that knowledge is created in the relationships built up by people that we can call, as a form of shorthand, 'teacher' and 'learner'. Knowledge is not fixed, is not certain; there are essential basic skills and base items of content that need to be absorbed before deep learning can take place – eg a concept of number, the structure of verbs in a foreign language, computational skills and so on – but once these foundations are established, then each person will create his or her own knowledge, her or his own reality. The teacher believes that the student already has important and worthwhile knowledge, and that the role of the teacher is to help the student explore that knowledge, reorder parts of it, and in the interaction of experience and deeper understanding feeding on each other, the student extends knowledge continuously. In this view, knowledge lives within the student and the teacher; it is not an entity imposed from outside.

Teaching and learning as replication

Consider this crudest possible caricature of what might happen in a classroom – a teacher selects a topic from a scheme of work, presents information to a group of children using verbal presentation and written materials, the children then replicate the information in their own books and then further replicate the material through a test, exercises or a piece of writing. The teacher then passes judgment on the extent to which the levels of replication coincide with the original as presented.

The important issue here is that the whole process is one of circular replication and it is possible to be considered a highly effective teacher and pupil in terms of the accuracy of the replication which is achieved.

The child's own map

One of the major weaknesses of such an approach is that it totally ignores the individual pupil. It assumes that the pupil is *tabula rasa* waiting for the imprint of the teacher's selection of information. The assumption is, of course, totally wrong. Children bring to school an intricate mind-map of their world. They have built up this map from birth, and it is a map of their reality. This point cannot be over-stressed. Over the years, through the immediate experiences of daily life, through the patterns of family life, through stories and observations, nonsense verse and TV, they have built a very clear map of reality. That map is their world, the basis upon which they act.

The teacher faced with 30 different maps cannot ignore them if he or she wants those children to learn. That teacher needs to get to know what those maps look like. Otherwise, the children will very quickly learn the 'school game'. That game is to remember that what the teacher says is important, repeat it back when asked, but not to let it impinge in any way on the carefully constructed map. There has been a very great deal of research into what students really believe despite having been through, and successfully so, education systems which have taught them something entirely opposed to their central beliefs. There were graduates of MIT who still believed that two forces were acting on a coin once it had left the thumb after flicking; graduates of a teaching hospital in South Africa who were convinced Lamarkians despite passing all the examinations in which they showed acceptance and understanding of Darwinism; primary children who knew that the sun was closer to the earth in summer despite what their teacher said, because they had experienced getting too hot as they got closer to a fire. We have all experienced that solid rejection of 'facts' which go against our deepest beliefs. Teaching which ignores the realities of the children will be rejected as surely as any graft which attempts to ignore the body's immune system. Gardner (1991, pp152 *et seq*, 169 *et seq*) gives a number of vivid examples of what happens if the teacher ignores what the student brings to the class, what mind-map is in place.

Many of the world's educational systems are posited on one basic premise – the possibility of the transfer of information and its faithful regurgitation, and its value. Perkins (1992, pp31 and 35) characterises this approach as naive theories of education and he identifies two:

1   learning is a matter of accumulating a large repertoire of facts and routines;

2   success in learning depends on ability much more than effort.

This naive approach leads to the nightmare vision of education as a game of Trivial Pursuit in which those who can remember the most facts are considered the most able. In fact, of course, this is precisely the premise on which most educational systems operate: the definition of a body of knowledge (ie a National Curriculum) and incremental, knowledge-based learning. What is missing from this formulation is any conceptualisation of learning for understanding. This is not to say that learning and understanding do not take place, but rather that they are incidental or accidental.

The capacity to learn

Our central contention in this book is that the key to personal survival, success and happiness in a rapidly changing world is the capacity to learn. Processing knowledge is a necessary component of an educational system but it is limited and constrained, and in turn is limiting and constraining. Eighteenth-century agricultural methods would work if they were applied today. However, they would almost certainly result in mass starvation. The continued application of outmoded views of what constitutes learning and knowledge is likely to lead to spiritual and economic starvation for individuals and nations.

Barriers to learning

It is intriguing to reflect on the reasons for the obstinate survival of the belief in the primacy of the transmission of knowledge as constituting learning. Two reasons can be advanced. First, there is a prevailing consensus about what constitutes the educational process. Second, there is an absence of a comprehensive understanding of the learning process. This section deals with the first of these reasons.

It is difficult to isolate the components of the concept of education in our schools. However, a number of significant features can be identified.

IQ

The British love of hierarchy is nowhere more deeply manifested than in the deference to IQ. At best IQ is a measure of logical intelligence, mental agility and the ability to solve a limited range of problems. At worst it is a denial of the validity of the abilities of the many by concentrating on the knack of being able to process a very limited and specific area of knowledge. The dominance of this narrow view of intelligence has a number of negative effects. It acts as a spurious legitimation for selection, it consolidates limited modes of assessment and it sets an artificial constraint on the potential for development of the majority.

Quite apart from the cultural and statistical problems with IQ testing, there is the contentious notion that there is a generic intellectual ability which is preordinate in its significance and specifically related to the capacity to learn. Significantly, most intelligence tests are based on convergent thinking which reinforces the notion of replication mentioned above. The use of IQ testing is not as ubiquitous as it once was, but there is still the impression left in many minds that it is testable and fixed.

Gardner (1993) has developed the most powerful critique of the dominance of a unifactoral definition of intelligence:

Adapting the appealing distinction of the Greek poet Archilochus, one can contrast those who view all intellect as a piece (let us call them 'hedgehogs'), with those who favor its fragmentation into several components (the 'foxes'). The hedgehogs not only believe in a singular inviolable capacity which is the special property of human beings; often as a corollary, they impose the condition that each individual is born with a certain amount of intelligence, and that we as individuals can in fact be rank-ordered in terms of our God-given intellect or I.Q. So entrenched is this way of thinking – and talking – that most of us lapse readily into rankings of individuals as more or less 'smart', 'clever' or 'intelligent'.

We are faced with education systems dominated by hedgehogs determined to perpetuate the hedgehog hegemony whose response to foxes is to curl up into a tight ball and be extremely prickly.

Goleman (1996, p34) identifies the central problem with such a myopic definition of intelligence:

One of psychology's open secrets is the relative inability of grades, I.Q., or SAT scores, despite their popular mystique, to predict unerringly who will succeed in life. . . . At best, I.Q. contributes about 20% to the factors that determine life success, which leaves 80% to other forces.

This finding might help to explain the somewhat limited contribution of hedgehogs to the sum total of human experience. However, as Rose (1996, p18) argues, the advocates of I.Q. are perpetuating a number of myths:

a. *There is a thing called 'intelligence'; intelligence tests measure it, and these tests yield a single figure; that figure, the person's I.Q., shows the ratio of that person's 'intelligence' to that of the general population.*

b. *Intelligence is a relatively fixed property of the brain, and individual differences are largely heritable.*

c. *Populations differ in their average I.Q. score. In the US, blacks score on average lower than whites, and in both the US and the United Kingdom, the working class lower than the middle class.*

d. *These differences are so great that 'the environment' cannot account for them, and therefore differences between groups are also inherited.*

Propositions a, b, and d are false. Proposition c is true, though for scientifically trivial, albeit socially profound, reasons.

Rose argues that the factors that make up an individual's abilities cannot be reduced to a single number which is then subject to the same statistical patterns as that person's height. Such an idea is palpable nonsense.

Until such time as humans live in a society in which social barriers restricting relationships between individuals from different ethnic and social groups no longer exist, the estimates (of I.Q.) are as scientifically meaningless as they are socially and politically pernicious. (Rose, 1996, p19)

It is worth reflecting on the extent to which our education system both in structural and in operational terms is based on the mythology of the possibility of measuring difference between people in terms of vocabulary, numerical and analogical reasoning and pattern recognition. The notion of a 'normal distribution curve', dividing humanity into predictable and fixed percentiles, remains pervasive – a triumph of arithmetical neatness over human experience.

The reification of knowledge

It seems almost disingenuous to question the primacy of knowledge in an education system, yet this is probably the major barrier to an understanding of learning. Most education systems are founded on the basis of the transmission of knowledge – usually manifested in a curriculum which is, in turn, fragmented into syllabuses and schemes of work. Such an approach has an impact on assessment which is largely concerned with the extent to which the student can reproduce the items of information.

A number of issues emerge from this situation. First, as has been said at the beginning of the chapter, there is a very great deal of pressure from the government to accept its version of what constitutes the material that our children have to imbibe, and the testing system and the league tables all add to this pressure. Some schools are having to move away from previously held positions against their best professional beliefs.

There is also, as has been stated, a profound misunderstanding of the word 'knowledge'. What is posited as knowledge is in fact information; not until the individual has absorbed the information, adapted it to the schemata already in his or her mind and discarded that which does not fit, only then can the individual be said to have 'knowledge'. Knowledge is created, not transmitted. Third, and for the moment allowing the general interpretation of the word 'knowledge', serious questions have to be raised about the integrity of the knowledge that is being transmitted. The history, science and so on that are taught at various ages are often so diluted that they have to be relearnt on several occasions in order to make them even partially meaningful to the individual pupil.

Fourth, there are serious doubts that the information being taught is actually correct – the myths of English history are a classic example of this. Very few curricula admit to the contingency of information, and subjects are taught with an absolute authority and conviction. Dr James Appleberry, the President of the American Association of State Colleges and Universities, said recently that:

> the sum total of humankind's knowledge has doubled at least every five years since [1965]. And by the year 2000, 97% of what is known at that time will have been discovered or invented since those of us reading this article were born. It's further projected that by the year 2020, knowledge or information will double every 73 days.

Even this statement makes the assumption that one can quantify knowledge; in the 'networked society', with limitless information available to anyone at any time, the main burden on people in general, and on our students in particular, will be to learn the techniques, the question-posing skills, that will enable them to make knowledge out of the welter of information. Imposing a curriculum based on no philosophical underpinning, and made up of slabs of information of dubious value, is dangerously asynchronous.

More worrying still is that modern technology means that there is no need to transmit information from teacher to pupil. Some classrooms still operate on the hypothesis that information is generally restricted in its availability and that therefore its recording is the most important educational activity. It would seem that some teachers still find it difficult to accept that information is now a given; the prime objective for the time the child is in school is for him or her to learn how to use the information, and above all how to make linkages, see the Gestalt and thus to move towards deep learning. The control of access to information and the primacy of the subject combine to limit the time available for such deep learning.

Assessment and its effect on learning

The opportunities for learning are even more constrained given the modes of assessment that are generally employed. If the curriculum is given the status of a canon, with political, social and moral functions, then assessment will inevitably be focused on establishing degrees of correctness. Thus a teacher's response to a student's work will be in binary terms – right or wrong – and such an attitude has disturbing echoes of Plato:

> If a man cannot define the Form of the Good and distinguish it clearly from anything else, and then defend it against all comers, not merely as a matter of opinion but in strict logic, and come through with his argument unshaken, you would not say that

he knew what Absolute Good was, or indeed any other good. Any notion such a man has is based on opinion rather than knowledge, and he is living in a dream . . . (1965, p303)

Most curricula are based on the notion of an 'Absolute Good' and tests and examinations are by and large concerned with defining 'the Form of the Good'. While there is something reassuring about this classical confidence, we now live in a far more complex world made up of processes which each have

a complex adaptive system [which] acquires information about its environment and its own interactions with that environment, identifying regularities in that interaction, condensing those regularities into a kind of 'schema' as model, and acting in the real world on the basis of that schema . . . . Each of us humans functions in many different ways as a complex adaptive system. (Gell-Mann, 1994, p17)

The process of formulating a schema is a learning process, which itself is a complex adaptive system. The contingent nature of knowledge has to be the basis for any curriculum rather than the notion that there can be a codified 'Absolute Good' for all areas of human activity. If knowledge is presented as an absolute, then the process of transmitting and receiving it must inevitably be presented as an absolute. Hence the confidence of Ofsted pronouncements about teaching at the expense of caution about learning.

Significantly, Bloom (1953) describes application, comprehension and knowledge as lower levels of thinking, and evaluation, synthesis and analysis as higher order. It is worth reflecting on the extent to which most existing curricula are located on lower levels of thinking.

School organisation

It may seem perverse in the extreme to characterise the way in which schools are organised as a barrier to learning. Yet it will be readily apparent that schools are postulated on the premises discussed in the previous two sections – the hierarchy of intelligence and the transmission of information. The two most obvious manifestations of schools' being so organised are the use of cohort-based chronological progression together with ability grouping, and the compartmentalisation into subject teaching.

Chronological lock-step

The notion of uniform chronological progression dominates the sequencing of educational experiences, notably in the National Curriculum, Key Stages and related assessments. Deviations from the perceived 'normal' continuity are treated as charming or freakish aberrations. However, the range of differences in any group of children is far more notable than the similarities. In fact it would be fair to say that the differences are the important factors to be taken into consideration by the teacher.

As was noted in Chapter 2, a class of children might cover a spread of seven years in terms of mathematical ability, and the same class might cover a spread of six years in reading ability, with some children's reading ability being two years behind their chronological age. Gender also has an impact, with boys and girls being quite sharply differentiated at different ages in terms of their relative progress in a number of conceptual areas. Despite all these considerable variations, they will all be in the same class, and will all be deemed ready to take the same test on the same day. Clearly, such grouping has a very great deal to do with administrative convenience, and in previous times reliance on a narrow range of information (the textbook and limited access to the library) also imposed this form of grouping. A focus on learning, rather than adult convenience, and the ubiquity of information would urge schools to look again at the underlying rationale for the class arrangements.

Chronology and Piaget

Much of this deference to chronology can be attributed to the theoretical justifications advanced by Piaget. There can be no doubting the importance of Piaget in creating an understanding of the sequence of intellectual and moral development. Gardner (1991, pp28–9), however, identifies four major concerns with the Piagetian world view. First, Piaget put forward the notion that development consists of a series of qualitative shifts in representation and understanding, whereas in fact many of them are present at birth or in early infancy and do not follow an extended developmental sequence. Second, Piaget believed in a parallel development of the different domains; Gardner argues from 'copious' evidence that the domains are in fact independent of each other and the structures of the mind 'evolve in different directions and at different paces'.

Third, Gardner argues that Piaget's work is almost entirely focused on scientific and numerical competence; in the final analysis, development for Piaget consisted in the evolution of the understanding of number. Finally, Gardner challenges Piaget's view that later modes of knowing eradicate earlier ones. 'For the most part, children's earliest conceptions and misconceptions endure throughout the school era.' Equally significant is Gardner's contention that once formal schooling is over, the earliest views may well re-emerge. Gardner concludes his discussion by drawing a powerful analogy between the development of children and that of computers:

> The serial, one-step-at-a-time computers of the past appear to be on their way out as models of the mind ... they are being replaced by parallel distributed systems that, brain-like, carry out many small quasi-independent computations at the same time ... the child postulated by information processors in the 1990s is a very different child from the one underlying the research of the 1970s or 1980s. (pp31–2)

What emerges from this critique is anxiety about the development of the majority of children being postulated on the basis of generic, sequential progression. Every teacher knows that such a neat progression is not true; in fact one of the 'skills' of the teacher is to accommodate a wide range of development within a standardised programme. The inexorable march of successive academic years takes no account of the relative development of the children in them.

Learning and subject boundaries

The subordination of individual differences in terms of chronology is exacerbated by the parallel emphasis on subjects, discrete areas of information. While we accept totally the importance and validity of areas of human experience and understanding, we have to raise a fundamental question about their relationship to learning. In fact it could be argued that 'learning a subject' is a paradox. Learning how to deploy knowledge is a very different proposition. Of course, learning cannot take place in a vacuum, but the primacy of subject knowledge in schools can only compromise the potential for learning. The separate subjects in the curriculum indicate a particular mind-set, and that mind-set holds that knowledge is made up of a number of small, separate pieces of information. The modernist desire always to reduce the topic in question to items, and the concurrent belief that the whole is merely the sum of the parts, inform the attitude to the curriculum. Breaking down 'knowledge' into sections labelled 'History', 'Biology', 'English Literature' and so on, and then further breaking these down into small sections, is seen as the easiest way for the children to absorb the warehouse of knowledge that is mandated. Such an attitude towards what students have to imbibe ensures that students believe that learning is the accumulation of more and more bits of information.

Beare and Slaughter (1993) make the point very powerfully:

> Not surprisingly because of its origins, the whole education establishment operates in that same bits-and-pieces approach which characterised the scientific method. For example, to construct the curriculum of secondary and primary schools, and also in universities, we break human knowledge down into disciplines, subjects and courses; and we allocate those specialisations to people who are trained in particular areas of knowledge. We make the assumption that the parts will add up to a coherent whole, and that the whole is indeed merely the sum of the parts. The important point here is that schools faithfully reproduce this distorted world-view, both in what they teach and also in the very ways in which the learning process is conceived of, organised, and delivered. It permeates the texture of education. Its influence is visible in the artificially produced competition in schools, in an infatuation with marks and grades, in the scramble for status created by hierarchies of schools, in the reduction of pupils to statistics, in the creation of 'experts', and in the absence of any credible future perspective.

A further significant manifestation of this compartmentalisation and non-linkage of information is the secondary school timetable which can have the following characteristics:

- activity constrained by artificial periods of time which have no known correlation with any learning process (the 40-minute lesson);
- random sequencing of subjects;
- block grouping of pupils based on one-dimensional criteria (ie intelligence or ability);
- an emphasis on teaching to 'get through' syllabuses and schemes of work;
- the design of activities to fit the time available rather than the needs of the children or the topic.

There is little doubt that the National Curriculum in England and Wales, and the Northern Ireland Curriculum, have done much to reinforce these features and move them into the primary school. However, it must be stated that (in our experience) all of these factors were present in schools long before the National Curriculum. For secondary schools, external examinations at 16+ and 18+ were the most significant factors in determining the daily experiences of students and these were in turn largely specified by higher education which was, and is, made up of jealously guarded subject areas.

However, we are equally aware of an astonishing variety of contemporary responses to these external requirements. Schools and classrooms are often highly distinctive and there are many examples of remarkably creative and innovative practices. They are, unfortunately, not the norm. They are not the norm because of the perception of teachers as to what their role is. This perception has been forced on them by a concatenation of years of blame and haranguing by politicians and the media, and by a public misunderstanding as to what sort of education our children need in order to thrive in the next century.

Teacher Perceptions

Our purely personal and anecdotal experience is that leaders, managers and teachers in schools are often extremely uncomfortable with the relationship between what, on the one hand, they are constrained to do and, on the other, the conceptualisation of the learning of the individual child.

Rogers (1983, p23) provides one possible explanation:

In the first place, many an instructor [sic] during all her professional training and experience, has been conditioned to think of herself as the expert, the information giver, the keeper of order, the evaluator of products, the examination giver, the one who, at the end, formulates that goal of all 'education' – the grade.

This view is reinforced by the research carried out by Strauss and Shilany (1994, p467). They found that in teachers' views

. . . the object of pedagogy is to get external subject matter into the place in the mind where knowledge is stored . . .

When teachers spoke about how they would teach children certain content, they typically began speaking about learning in terms of the subject matter they wanted to teach. They believed that knowledge in various disciplines differs in kind, abstractions and complexity. One of their chief concerns was about how to package content knowledge for their pupils so that it can be learned.

There are, of course, many explanations for this situation. A range of factors may be identified:

- the historic experience of teachers – i.e. a form of cultural reproduction in which their own experience is a key determining factor in the conceptualisation of their role;

- the emphasis in teacher training (a highly significant term) on academic knowledge, traditionally disseminated, and training in teaching strategies. The notion of learning is marginalised into theoretical studies of the psychology of education;

- the imperatives of the National Curriculum and external examinations which emphasise the transmission of content within a rigid time sequence;

- the organisation of schools into subject areas and the extension into the timetable of a subject-based organisation;

- the culture of teaching.

This last point is worth developing in more detail. In her study of a secondary school's humanities scheme, Buswell (1988, p124) identifies the pressure for standardised approaches:

Given a large and heterogeneous staff, curriculum packaging allied to individualised pedagogy can be a more coercive form of control than reliance on a unified belief system or assumed homogeneity ... One humanities teacher, in describing the scheme, said, 'We're just glorified clerks now!'

The significance of this is in the emphasis on standardisation through the production of materials with associated patterns of assessment which, taken together, help to guarantee pedagogic practice, without reference to learning outcomes. The scheme created a situation where:

The text directed pupils to books and information kept elsewhere, which was part of the aim of teaching them to 'learn'. But a 'particular answer' was still required, and finding it became a complicated orienteering process conducted through the printed word ... The emphasis in all the units was on following precise instructions and replicating what someone else had produced ... (Buswell, 1988, p127)

The plethora of published and school-based schemes has the effect of creating a culture of 'routine occupational work' (Buswell, 1988, p128) which facilitates control but denies the development of the individual and effectively deskills and diminishes the teacher. Not only are pupils controlled, but teachers are also subject to external constraints. These constraints may point to a significant tension between what a school aspires to do in terms of learning and the actual experience of both pupils and teachers. The external constraints push the school into actions which run counter to the best interests of the child in terms of his or her learning. 'We have to get through the material'; tests have to be taken on time; children have to be processed through the school day. Control becomes the overriding imperative. Indeed, it has been argued by a number of writers that the curriculum, in its widest sense, is an imposed control mechanism, designed primarily to produce conformist young people.

In a literate culture, we see one of the main tasks of education as being to introduce our children to the texts that they will encounter. Children need to know the functions of a variety of texts. However, in too many classrooms, what should be an exploration of how text, readers and individual experience produce a variety of meanings becomes instead an imposition of one meaning: the mere transmission of information. The purpose behind such diminution of the possible outcomes is not only to ensure that children come very early to the understanding that texts have a 'right' and a 'wrong' meaning, and that their task is to quarry the right one. The purpose is wider: it is to ensure that children learn to be conformist in their attitude to social conventions in general. Many of the structures in schools – the time-table, the control of movement, the strict hierarchical lines of authority – combine with the limited ways of handling text to ensure that a politically correct conformism is inculcated from an early age.

A control culture

There are many manifestations of this overriding concern with control, with 'keeping the machinery going'. Among them are:

- the ratio of teacher-talk to pupil-talk;
- the relative number of teacher–class, teacher–pupil and pupil–pupil interactions;
- the proportions of time spent on negotiation of lesson outcomes and the means of achieving them;
- the amount of time devoted to individual as against whole-class review;
- the number of times the lesson plan is deviated from in response to pupil interest;
- the nature of assessment.

To these factors must be added a range of others which are more symbolic in nature but nevertheless help to reinforce a culture of control, eg the arrangements for eating, the existence of a dress code, the use of names (first or second and who uses which to whom) and exemptions from standard practice. This last is particularly significant as nothing reinforces a control culture so strongly as the creation of special cases. Thus, in schools, the culture of teaching is very closely aligned with a control culture, which in turn is identified with a hierarchical and highly differentiated organisation. None of these manifestations of control have very much to do with learning.

Control versus discipline

Let there be no misunderstanding. There is a very considerable difference between, on the one hand, 'controls' which are, in the main, externally imposed and externally monitored and, on the other, that internally accepted discipline which arises within an interpretive community (see Chapter 7). This difference needs to be stressed. Learning will not take place unless the consciously accepted discipline of the learner working alongside the teacher/coach, and the discipline of what is being learnt, cohere. Control is imposed for administrative convenience, for the benefit of the controllers; discipline is built by the learners in order to learn.

Towards a definition of learning

It is not our intention in this section to produce a single, authoritative definition of learning – we doubt if this is possible or even desirable. Indeed we would wish to stress the central importance of a school's developing a common and shared understanding of the word 'learning' which is meaningful to that community and applicable to that particular context. What follows is an attempt to help map what the components of such an understanding might be.

Modes of assessment and learning

It may be helpful to begin with an outline of what learning is, and of how different modes of assessment either help or hinder the form of learning that we need to see in our schools and colleges.

Let us pose three statements:

'I have learned how to boil an egg.'

'I am learning to speak French.'

'I have learned French.'

The first and the second stand, of course, for a wide range of learned items or areas of learning – the number of angles in a triangle, the date of the Norman Conquest, the stages in passing a Bill and its becoming an Act. It is easy to accept the meaningfulness of the first two statements, and in no small measure this ease is due to there being little difficulty in assessing the truth or otherwise of the statement. The last statement is more problematic.

To assess if I have learnt how to boil an egg, I merely have to present the assessor with en egg that is not too runny and not too solid. The assessment is unifactoral. I do not have to explain the origin of the egg, nor the types of feeding necessary to produce a sound egg, nor the physics involved in the heating of the water. The assessment is closely focused on the end-product and its matching the specification set down before I started to boil it.

With the second, the assessment is a little more complex, but not much. I show the assessor my notebooks, a list of the books I am reading, a list of the tapes I am listening to, demonstrate my ability to speak a few sentences, show a capacity to run through an irregular verb or two, translate some material. The length of the assessment would depend in part on the amount of time I have spent learning French, but it would not need to be very lengthy. I would not be asked about the political situation in France, how the advent of the hyper-marché had impacted on the average French village, how young men court young women in contemporary France, or a dozen other questions about life in France. They would not be germane to finding the answer to the question: 'Is this person learning French?' The focus for this assessment would be the same as the first – the end-product.

The last statement, however, would demand a most complex and lengthy assessment. The assessor would need to see the student in a number of situations, to see how he or she coped with a variety of relationships, to note the depth of the interest in contemporary France. The emphasis in this case would not be the end-product; the perfect tense is, in this case, open-ended with a hint of continuity about it, and in any case, even if closed, would encompass so wide a territory that no end-product test could encompass it. The emphasis would be on the process, and the process involves the student being observed and talked with in a number of relationships, in a number of locations and encounters. Indeed, after a time, it would be difficult to make a cut-off point between coach/teacher and assessor; it might be argued that the coach/assessor would be the ideal, with a validating body in the background for quality assurance. It is worth stressing also that this assessment would not be time- or location-bound.

It is worth comparing that idealised way of assessing the student-in-progress with the current, narrowing, way of assessing our sixth-form students. The present way of assessing, say, a sixth-form student of English Literature would be regarded as bizarre in any but the educational world. Consider a student, Susan, who has been studying English Literature for 'A' level for nearly 18 months. Among other texts, she has been studying *Hamlet*. She knows that at the end of the course she will need to prove that she 'knows' *Hamlet*. Over the two years, she has built up a good rapport with her teacher and with the rest of the group. They have frequently discussed the play, and been together to a film and a theatre version of it. As the 'A' level assessment system stands at present, however, she has to prove her knowledge of the play by focusing on writing one or two essays on it. The essay titles will be chosen by someone who knows neither her nor her teacher, and who does not ask her what she wants to demonstrate or how, and the paper will be marked by someone who does not know the questioner nor the teacher nor the class. The grade will be awarded solely on the product, the essay(s) that Susan has managed to write in the two or three hours allotted. The marker will never discuss the findings with Susan. So much of what she has experienced has been sidelined; the play as a piece of theatre has been reduced to a text-in-study; her changed ways of looking at her world as a result of the impact of the experience are irrelevant. What this system in fact says to the students is: 'Let's focus on what we can get across to the examiner in a couple of essays. That way lies success.' That some teachers and students rise above such a banal approach to literature is a testimony to them.

In any other walk of life the assessed and the assessor decide together on the area under scrutiny. Together they will look at ways in which the assessment will be carried out, and together they will discuss the outcomes.

An alternative assessment

Susan could demonstrate her knowledge and involvement with the play by choosing to act a scene – say, the scene before the play within the play – with a friend in the role of Hamlet, and preface her acting with a spoken commentary, conclude with another and, if very sophisticated, break into her performance to explain the significance of the action or the words in the light of past or future segments of the play. She could support this performance with a portfolio of work garnered during the year, and the teacher and Susan could, also during the year, video-tape conversations which record her deepening interest in the play and the impact that it is having on her. All this could be discussed with an external assessor through a video link. The whole emphasis would be on assessing as wide a range of reactions and knowledges and insights as possible, and, essentially, looking at process as well as product.

A number of points arise from these contrasting modes of assessment. First, my learning will be shaped by the form of assessment that I know will be employed. Ramsden, quoted by Willis (1993), puts it well:

> Evidence now exists to show students' interests, attitudes to studying, and approaches to academic tasks are strongly related to their experiences of teaching and assessment.

In very blunt terms – in education, measuring changes what is being measured.

Second, approaches to learning combine both the product and the process of learning. One therefore cannot consider what a student has learnt without considering *how* he or she learnt it.

Third, a hierarchical system of assessment will focus on that Platonic dichotomy mentioned earlier – is it right or wrong? To be able to focus on the process, there will need to be a partnership between student and coach/ teacher, not a hierarchy. In such a partnership, assessment stops being something you do to other people who are in a lower position, but rather becomes an interactive dialogue between student and coach, a dialogue that is essential in providing the insights into what can ensure and improve learning. Together, student and coach look at both the student's learning and the coach's activities, and in an equality of involvement there will be a two-way investigation of what has been going on during the period under scrutiny. The style of this assessment can be summed up as a joint activity exploring the relationship between student and coach to ensure that both achieve the jointly established aim.

Fourth, and possibly most importantly, the majority of assessments of the core areas of the curriculum focus on two intelligences – linguistic intelligence and logico-mathematical intelligence. Gardner's work (1991) on multiple intelligences showed that the other five intelligences – spatial, musical, kinesthetic, interpersonal and intrapersonal – are all used to different degrees and at different times by individuals to make sense of their world and to represent reality. The overriding form of assessment in schools – the written paper, the written test – denies the validity of other forms of learning, other ways of interpreting the world, and restricts the meanings that the student can make.

Categories of learning

At this point it might be helpful to give a categorisation of learning. This categorisation builds on the outline in Chapter 2. It was created by Saljo and quoted in Dolin and Ingerslev (1996). He breaks down teaching into five levels, but a number of writers in this field have since added on a sixth:

A. Increase in knowledge

B. Memorising

C. Acquisition of facts, to be retained and used when necessary

D. The abstraction of meaning

E. An interpretative process aimed at understanding reality

F. Changing as a person

The first three items can be labelled 'shallow learning' and the second three 'deep learning'. The shallow learning items do not affect me-as-person. Those forms of learning enable me to pass tests, to win at Trivial Pursuit, to survive and even thrive in those schools and colleges that demand no more of me. The forms of teaching and assessment that focus on items of information and on the end-product are served by and encourage these three forms of learning. The major problems are that they do not demand very much of my involvement, and, more importantly, that success in them does not mean that I have learnt anything. Getting ten out of ten in a series of end-product tests is no guarantee of learning. This approach to assessment and teaching has thrown up a very great deal of evidence that shows that not only do students not understand key concepts in the subject, but that they can be more confused by the end of the course than they were at the beginning. There is the example from some research by Dahlgren quoted by Gibbs (1992) which showed that students at the end of their first year of an economics course ended by having poorer quality of understanding of several concepts than they had at the beginning. What was particularly interesting was that results on a conventional examination revealed none of this failure. Gardner (1993, Chapter 8) gives a number of fascinating examples of the results of superficial learning.

The other three forms of learning – D, E and F – require the student's involvement. In these activities the student begins to pull the disparate bits of information together and begins to perceive meaning in them. For example, a series of facts about the Divine Right of Kings can make sense, make meaning to the student, only when there has been that conceptual Eureka moment at which the student feels deep inside the powerlessness of the commoner faced with the total power of a ruthless God-King.

The next stage comes when the student begins to put that insight together with an insight into the writings of Tom Paine, another into the origins of the French Revolution and possibly some reading of Prudhon, and begins to relook at his or her world and at how power is distributed. The student's reality is changed. As that reality changes, so does the student as a person. He or she can, to use a cliché, 'never be the same again'. That is deep learning.

From shallow to deep

The problem for schools is to move from shallow to deep learning. So much of what we learn in schools impinges on us as a person not one whit. Students imbibe vast quantities of 'facts', and live their lives entirely unaffected by them. That learning is not only shallow, it is also symbolic; it is needed to pass on to the next stage, at which point it is forgotten or rejected. An enormous amount of teacher and student energy has been expended to little or no purpose. There are, however, difficulties in moving away from shallow learning.

In the first section of this chapter we sought to set out what we believe to be the barriers to real learning. We recognise that many of these are axiomatic to many prevailing definitions of the nature and purpose of education. However, as we demonstrate in Chapter 2, there is enough alternative practice in schools to give us the confidence to argue for an understanding of the learning process that is already available but not necessarily widely practised. One of the problems with talking about learning is that it is highly individualised and subjective. There is a natural temptation to focus on that which can be easily discussed and controlled. However:

> We must learn to measure what we value rather than valuing what we can easily measure. (National Indicators' Panel, 1992)

The process of learning

What follows is an attempt to delineate what we can understand about the process of learning. Sacks (1995, ppxiii–xiv), when he was recovering from an injury to his shoulder, provides a powerful model of the learning process:

> *I am writing this with my left hand, although I am strongly right-handed . . . I write slowly, awkwardly, but more easily, more naturally, with each passing day. I am adapting, learning, all the while . . . now I walk differently, I have discovered a new balance. I am developing different patterns, different habits . . . a different identity one might say. Though some of my adaptations are deliberate, planned, and some are learned through trial and error . . . most have occurred by themselves, unconsciously, by reprogramming, and adaptations of which I know nothing.*

Sacks concludes this analysis by pointing out that the process of recovery is uniquely individualistic, made up of learning, synthesising and adapting. Although there are standard procedures and norms to measure progress, the transition to full recovery can be understood only in personal terms. We would argue that the learning process follows the same path.

Just as the concept of health – the product of recovery – is multi-faceted, so is learning. When Sacks had completed his recovery he (it is to be hoped) *felt* well and was also able to *do* things. This combination of a personal sense of well-being and the capacity to act is central to our understanding of learning. There has to be a balance of a personal and emotional sense of self as well as purely practical outcomes. As we have argued in the first section of this chapter, much of what passes for learning in schools is focused on a narrow and profoundly instrumental notion of what constitutes learning – the ability to replicate. A powerful antidote to the model is provided by Gardner (1993) in his theory of multiple intelligences. He argues that

> *. . . if we are to encompass adequately the realm of human cognition, it is necessary to include a far wider and more universal set of competencies than has ordinarily been considered. And it is necessary to remain open to the possibility that many – if not most – of these competencies do not lend themselves to measurement by standard verbal methods, which rely heavily on a blend of logical and linguistic abilities.*

> *. . . and intelligence is the ability to solve problems or create products that are valued within one or more cultural settings.* (pxiv)

Gardner argues for a view of intelligence that is humane, respects differences and shuns an artificially created hierarchy of significance. Instead of the prevailing emphasis on logical-mathematical intelligences, Gardner argues that we need to be aware of six other intelligences: linguistic intelligence, musical intelligence, spatial intelligence, physical/kinesthetic intelligence, inter-personal intelligence, intrapersonal intelligence. Given the British love of hierarchies, such a list must be protected from being ordered into a hierarchy of significance. Gardner (1993, p68) argues:

It is a mistake to try to compare intelligences on all particulars; each must be thought of as a system with its own roles ... Even though the eye, the heart and the kidneys are all bodily organs, it is a mistake to try to compare these organs in every particular; the same restraint should be observed in the case of intelligences.

Equally he says that 'Intelligences are not to be thought of in evaluative terms.' This view clearly has profound implications for the way that state education systems perceive the nature, purpose and outcomes of education. It is not enough to argue that a curriculum has balance in terms of a range of subjects; if the subjects are taught and assessed in more or less the same way, then the balance is spurious. It is much more to do with the definitions and measurement of outcomes, with the range of assessment methods and the relative significance attached to each component. In essence, however varied the list of subject labels, the pupils' experiences will be reduced to linguistic and logical criteria through a reductionist assessment procedure. Learning is thus constricted to a limited definition of intelligence which denies the existence, let alone the validity, of the multiplicity of intelligences.

It is the tragedy of much of our schooling that we are led to think that logical intelligence is the only type that matters. Any observation of our friends and colleagues in later life will prove that the other intelligences are at least as important, if not more so. We should train ourselves not to ask 'How intelligent is he/she?' but 'Which intelligence does he/she have most of?' (Handy, 1989, p17)

Quality learning

Perhaps the most damning indictment of the limited definitions of intelligence is the concept of the 'slow learner' – an individual is categorised by relatively poor performance in one domain, and this label then becomes a generic classification influencing the whole of his or her subsequent education. If a broad view of intelligence is taken, then it becomes possible to see learning as a multi-faceted process with a number of components, each of which is significant. At this point it is worth giving Bowden's (quoted in Willis, 1993) definition of 'quality learning':

It is not simply increasing the store of knowledge, taking in and retaining (or no) more and more information. It is about searching for meaning, developing understanding and relating that understanding to the world around us. As a consequence, the world is seen differently and student conceptions have undergone change. Quality learning is about conceptual change – seeing the world differently is an essential outcome.

The ultimate criterion for learning has to be the extent to which personal change has taken place. In other words, has the individual changed his or her view of reality? Has the individual been enabled to do something differently, see something differently, hear new sounds, cope with a different range of people, readjust a value system? There are many situations where information

79

may appear to have been transmitted and received (all the answers in the test are right) but in fact there has been no impact on the Gestalt of the individual. Thus I may learn a poem, a list of dates, mathematical laws and so on, and be able to reproduce them to my teacher's total satisfaction, but I have not changed one iota; I have not been enabled to alter my view of the world at all. Such knowledge was described by Perkins (1992, p21) as inert or ritual knowledge. Such knowledge inevitably compromises the educational process, especially when most school systems assume a cumulative process of knowledge acquisition. The failure to internalise, or rather the induced failure to internalise, caused by an assessment system which emphasises the replication of disconnected data is symptomatic of a lack of understanding.

Understanding

If learning has taken place on an individual, subjective level, then it will be manifested in what Perkins (1992, p77) describes as 'understanding performances', ie the evidence that indicates the transition from knowing to understanding. These 'performances' will include the ability to:

- *explain* the topic in the person's own words;
- provide new *examples* of the topic at work;
- *apply* the acquired knowledge and skills to new, unknown situations;
- *justify* through the offering of evidence;
- *compare and contrast* with other situations;
- *contextualise* the knowledge;
- *generalise* into a broader context;
- *select the medium* (eg speaking, writing, music, movement etc) which can best demonstrate understanding.

Understanding is a matter of the creation of personal mental maps or models, the creation of one's reality. Think of the first few weeks in your present job – much of that time was spent building up a mental map of the school – layout, roles, personalities. However, the school does not exist as a site plan or as an organisational diagram; at the same time that you were finding your way about the school, literally, you were also developing an understanding of how it works, what the culture of the place is, by building your reality of the place, checking that reality against new data. In time, you built up a personal picture of the school that allowed you to *be* there – however, this was and will always be a subjective view, derived from public data but interpreted according to your personal history, your existing mind-set. You could exist and thrive in the school because you had created a personal understanding, which in turn gave you a meaning.

Furthermore, you were able to create your own mind-map of the school because you were able to abstract meaning from the information that you gathered. The process of creating personal meaning is very much one of abstraction – the ability to create meaning – ie the capacity to think. It does not matter what the topic that is being studied is – Keynesian economics, why some objects float and others sink, why a sonnet moves us, how to produce a particular tone on the cello or how to hop – we need certain thinking skills. When a student is given material which demands only retention or repetition of mechanical skills, then his thinking is not being expanded.

Exploring the mind map

It must be stressed that in order to know if a child has changed his or her mind-set, it is first essential that teacher and child together explore the mind-set that the child has brought to the class. Frequently teachers say that there is no time for such exploration, that the demands of the subject content are paramount. If this is so, then what is being said is that there is no time for learning. What is being said is that the transfer and retention (or no) of information is all that we can manage in schools. The argument we put forward is that unless time is taken to explore what the child brings to school and build on that, then not only are we reduced to information handlers, but children will not do as well in an aspect of the curriculum because solid foundations have not be established from the outset. Time taken to explore is not time wasted; it is essential to give child and teacher/coach the chance to know the starting point, build conceptual underpinnings and together settle the new knowledge onto the old so that a coherent totality is reached.

Conclusion

What we are saying has many implications in the search for effective learning. First and foremost, it cannot be stressed too strongly that the teaching–learning process is highly interactive, changing according to need, adaptable, flexible. At this point, the child needs direct instruction, and at that time to explore and experiment; at another point learning will come through dialogue, and at another through working with a group; at another point, there has to be a time of quiet reflection, and at another a helter-skelter pursuit of an all-absorbing topic. There can be no formula except that of focusing on the child's learning needs. It is fruitless to try to simplify the discussion about what goes on in the classroom by positing the false dichotomy of 'progressive' vs 'traditional' teaching. Wenham (1991) puts the argument cogently:

> These theories of education are largely ineffective; but not because they are inconsistent or unjustifiable. In certain circumstances, both have much to offer in terms of ideas to inform and organise classroom practice. They are ineffective because they make the same assumption: that it is possible to prescribe a pattern of activity which will lead to effective learning and development without knowing anything of

the individual pupils or the circumstances in which the teaching–learning process is to be undertaken. Educational theorists often appear to teachers as a medical practitioner might who prescribed a course of treatment without ever having met, conversed with or carried out a thorough diagnostic investigation of the patient.

Second, there has to be trust between teacher and taught. The child is not going to be open and discuss his or her thoughts, experiences and view of the world to someone felt to be unworthy or unaccepting of trust. Equally, the teacher has to trust the pupil, and show that trust. That trust has to be an unequivocal given. Trust is not earned; rather it is reciprocated. Third, the child and the teacher are, at different times and in different ways, going to be both teacher and learner. The child will learn from the teacher, but the teacher will learn from the child – there has to be an equality of interchange. Fourth, if deep learning means that over time the child is changed, so, equally, will the teacher be changed. It would be a strange person indeed who could help and enthuse the children in his or her classes fundamentally to explore their minds and change the way they understand their reality, and yet remain unchanged him- or herself.

Finally, both participants in this process must be clear and overt about what learning is and how it can be fostered and sustained. If someone is to be a good athlete, he or she is helped to improve their running technique, their skills in hurdling, their throwing of the discus. If someone is to be a champion swimmer, they will be helped to concentrate on technique and, most importantly, be taught about how their body works and how best to fine-tune it. Similarly, if we are to learn more easily and effectively, we need to explore the very many different ways people learn and find the one that suits us best; we need to know something about how the brain works, and how the body's workings, in particular its nutritional needs, affect our brains and how well or not they work. The dialogue between teacher and taught will be in part about opening up the process of learning for continual scrutiny, both learning from the other about what helps and what hinders the learning process.

Salient features of profound learning

- Before a new topic is started, time needs to be given to an exploration of the pupil's mind-map.
- Pupil and teacher are continuously aware of and discuss the processes of learning.
- Pupil and teacher will ensure that assessment procedures embrace process as well as product.
- Pupil and teacher together look for a variety of ways in which the learning can best be demonstrated.
- Pupil and teacher ensure that over a period of time all intelligences are stretched and engaged.

- The learner and the subject matter will be treated holistically.
- More is less – a deeper and more rigorous examination of less material will, over time, benefit the pupil's learning far more than a rush to cover a set quantity of material.
- Learning is triggered and sustained by curiosity.
- Learning need no longer be confined by the geography of the school or the limits of the school day.
- The purpose of learning is to enable the individual to change, grow and become autonomous.

Activities

What follows are some suggestions of what a school might undertake in order to begin to know what students and teachers believe 'learning' and 'teaching' to be. The assumption is that in most schools, learning is one of the core activities. Other core activities might be the provision of a stable environment for children; another might be to provide a learning environment for teachers; another might be to provide a focal point for the local community. It would be strange, however, to find a school for which learning was not a prime aim.

It is clearly impossible for a school to evaluate whether it is being successful in enabling children to learn if the teachers and pupils are at odds as to what constitutes good teaching and deep learning. It needs to be stressed that the student who accepts shallow learning will have a very different concept of what a good lesson is from the concept held by that student who is a deep learner. Similarly, a teacher who sees knowledge as fixed will structure the lesson and the learning outcomes of the students very differently from the teacher who sees knowledge as created. It will also be necessary to look at the forms of assessment that are generally used: the form of assessment predicts the form of learning.

What follows is not intended to be prescriptive, but merely provides hints towards a teaching/learning audit. The wording of the questionnaires (and we are indebted to Gibbs (1992)) needs to be adapted to the culture of the individual school. Most schools' aims contain references to the desire to help pupils learn. The need is to find out if the school community has a commonality in the meanings it assigns to the key words, and if not, to find out where the gaps are, and then to find ways to bridge them.

Pupil shadowing

The managers of a school need to know what the pupils experience on a day-to-day basis. That knowledge has to be first-hand to be of any true value. Shadowing is the only way to gather evidence of the individual's total school experience. For the purposes of this enquiry, the following questions might be considered:

1 How often does the pupil negotiate the lesson outcomes?

2 How often, and for how long, does the pupil discuss the *process* of the work with the teacher?

3 To what extent is the teacher aware of the preferred learning styles of each pupil in the class?

4 To what extent are those styles catered for?

5 If they are not, what are the blockages?

6 What is the ratio of praise to blame that the pupil receives during the day?

7 In the written comments on the pupil's work is the process and not merely the outcomes commented on?

8 Does the pupil know the criteria that the teacher uses in saying that a piece of work is 'good' or 'bad'?

9 To what extent does the assessment procedure examine and comment on the learning process?

10 What is the total length of time, during a school day, which the pupil has in on-task conversations with teachers?

11 To what extent is the pupil encouraged to find his/her own path through the topic/problem?

12 To what extent is the pupil encouraged to reflect on what he/she is involved in?

13 Over the period of a week/month, does the pupil encounter the opportunity to learn in a number of different styles (a minimum of six?)?

14 Over the period of a week/month, is the pupil given the opportunity to demonstrate competence in a number of different ways?

15 Are problems always assumed to have a solution?

16 Are all seven intelligences acknowledged?

17 Are pupils helped to find multiple paths through their learning, and encouraged to find their preferred way?

18 Are all seven intelligences given equal status?

19 Do pupil records refer to the dominant intelligence(s) and how it/they is/are being developed?

20 Do reports to parents refer to pupils' learning styles and how they are being supported?

Questionnaire for pupils

On a 1 to 5 scale (1 = total agreement; 5 = total disagreement), please rate the following statements:

1 A good teacher does most of the work in the classroom – we listen and take notes.

2 A good teacher makes all the decisions about what we learn, and when and how we learn.

3 A good teacher gives us a grade and this tells us if we have learnt well or not.

4 A good teacher selects all the topics that we have to cover.

5 A good teacher decides on the tests that will show if we have learnt the material or not.

6 A good teacher decides how we should present what we have learnt.

7 A good teacher always controls who speaks and when.

8 A good teacher tells us what resources we need.

An alternative questionnaire for pupils

On a 1 to 5 scale (1 = total agreement; 5 = total disagreement), please rate the following statements:

1 A good teacher sets an open climate for questioning and comment.

2 A good teacher makes a range of resources available and lets us choose.

3 A good teacher talks with us about different ways of approaching the topic.

4 A good teacher gives us the responsibility for choosing the learning goals.

5 A good teacher encourages us to show what we have learnt in the way we want.

6 A good teacher helps us see the whole picture.

7 A good teacher works alongside us.

8 A good teacher encourages us to think about and talk about what we are doing.

These two questionnaires could, of course, be merged.

A questionnaire for teachers

On a 1 to 5 scale (1 = total agreement; 5 = total disagreement), please rate the following statements:

1 My job is to get across the facts.

2 What the students need to know is in the textbooks and my worksheets.

3 Essentially, I have to be in control of the classroom.

4 I have to decide on the learning outcomes.

5 When the pupils write something, I look for whether they have the right answers.

6 It's up to me to decide on how the pupils show they have learnt something.

7 I have to be in charge of the resources.

8 The pupils do not need to know the end point; they just have to cope with each step.

9 If the pupils do not learn something, they just need to work harder.

10 There is a lot of material that the class must get through; that is my main objective.

5

■ ■ ■

Learning: The Variables

World is crazier and more of it than we think,
Incorrigibly plural.
(Louis MacNeice, *Snow*)

In this chapter, we want to identify and explore the many variables that impinge on an individual's learning. As with any process involving personal change, the outcome of learning will be significantly determined by the way in which these variables, some personal and intrinsic, some social and extrinsic, are managed. If schools are to focus on learning, then the key task of leadership and management is to create the most propitious circumstances in which the individual is able, is encouraged and indeed wants to learn – everything else is subordinate.

Managing the variables

The management of variables is a highly complex and demanding task and most of us, in ordering our own lives, seek to reduce and simplify them as far as is possible. We establish timetables and routines; we create pathways through our neighbourhood and town; we try to reduce distractions; we set up, consciously or unconsciously, priorities of tasks that we 'have' to get through during the day. The variables that may lead us to a chance wandering along the riverbank, to a long conversation followed by a relaxed lunch far from home may be tempting but are for the most part resisted because we would be 'failing in our duties' were we to indulge ourselves. In part this adherence to self-imposed restrictions is due to an element of Puritanical morality, in part because life is a lot simpler, even if less interesting, if we keep to a set of rules.

Organisations work in the same way by limiting the range of possibilities to be managed – the secondary school timetable is the classic exemplification of this simplification. However, as the timetable directly affects children's learning, there is a major, and unacceptable, price to be paid. By carefully circumscribing the paths that the child can take, by closing down the variables of time and location, by limiting the range of groups within which the child can be placed, shallow learning is the inevitable result. As Chapter 2 has demonstrated, learning, as opposed to being the recipient of teaching, is an individual and subjective phenomenon which has to result in the school recognising that the management of learning cannot be posited on homogeneous and linear models of cohort progression.

Focus on the individual

If schools are to have confidence that every individual is learning, then the basis for management has to be the individual as the focus of a number of variables. One of the most significant outcomes of the consumer movement has been the increased importance attached to individual choice. Indeed, quality is often associated with the degree to which the individual is able to exercise meaningful choice; making things 'bespoke' is the consumer ideal. The customer is satisfied to the extent to which he or she feels that their needs are being met on an individual basis. Organisations which are successful are managed so as to enhance opportunities for the customer to make an informed choice. In education, however, choice is severely constrained and often not even available in the most important elements. Effective learning requires choice in *how* I learn rather than *what* I learn.

Confidence is a central concept in this context. When I board an aircraft, I have confidence that everything that needs to be done to ensure a safe flight has been done. When I order food in a restaurant, I do so on the basis of confidence that the food is nutritious, the kitchen is hygienic, and that those who serve me will get the food to me unspoilt. In both cases, management exists to create the optimum circumstances. Schools can be confident about many things; they are almost always safe, orderly places in which a great many complex activities take place with a high degree of predictability. However, it might be that schools have confidence in the wrong things. There is a natural and understandable tendency to gravitate towards those things that can be so ordered and controlled that confidence is justified. If schools are to become learning communities, then there has to be confidence in the learning of the individual – not in the teaching of the class. The fact that such a change is difficult and complex because learning is not predictable does not excuse a reluctance to address the issues.

The first step in increasing confidence that individuals are learning is to attempt to identify the variables that have to be managed. We offer the following list, in no particular order of significance:

- learning styles;
- teaching strategies;

- prior knowledge;
- cognitive skills;
- social skills;
- feedback, recognition and reinforcement;
- neurological factors;
- health and diet;
- access to resources;
- intrinsic motivation;
- multiple intelligences;
- information technology.

Every individual learner is a product of those factors. Each factor will have a different importance and impact over time and context – some can be addressed directly whereas others are more elusive. For example, it is possible for a school to ensure that each child has access to the library whenever such access can help learning, but it is more difficult (perhaps impossible) to influence the diet. What this list does raise as an immediate practical issue is the extent to which learners understand themselves as learners, and how much the very considerable information that schools collect about pupils is used very precisely to help put in place the opportunities to match learning styles to the child's needs. The need for extensive and detailed diagnosis and then application of that diagnosis at the outset of any learning process is fundamental.

Diagnosis

The skill of a doctor is directly proportionate to his or her skills in diagnosing, and a return to health is the result of the highest possible correlation between diagnosis and treatment. Success in learning is equally the result of a three-stage diagnosis: first, a high level of understanding of what the learner's needs are; second, an analysis of the extent and the ways in which the factors in the list above impinge upon the learner; third, the selection of the optimum strategy. Few of us would accept a diagnosis from our doctor that did not involve detailed understanding of our particular symptoms and case history. The same medication cannot be prescribed to the whole waiting room; such prescriptions have to follow individual consultation. Difficult cases may require increasingly sophisticated diagnostic procedures. The analogy with the medical world is appropriate; the inability to learn is just as incapacitating as any physical disability.

The learner, of whatever age, needs a diagnostic profile of him- or herself as learner. To sustain the medical analogy – learners need some form of identification in order to make those with whom they come into contact aware of their needs. The implications of there being a lack of awareness of learning needs are that there will be inappropriate treatments which could do more harm than good. What is at issue is translating into practice schools' avowed concern with the whole child – in other words, establishing a holistic and integrative approach to learning which respects children as they are, that is as individuals, rather than as they might be, that is as items in categories.

Learning styles

It is highly symptomatic of the uncertainty about learning in schools and classrooms that while there is a great deal of research and literature relating to the activity of the teacher, there is relatively little on how children learn. At the most basic level, if the strategy of the teacher does not coincide with the learning style of the pupil, there will be a mismatch resulting in a lack of understanding. It may well be that the major cause of what teachers regard as inappropriate behaviour in classrooms is at least partially the result of this mismatch.

The best known analysis of learning styles is derived from the work of David Kolb and applied to management development by Peter Honey and Alan Mumford (1986). They identify four broad learning styles:

- *reflector:* learning by feeling and through experience;
- *theorist:* learning by watching – ideas are important;
- *pragmatist:* learning by thinking – enjoys problem-solving;
- *activist:* learning by doing.

These styles are highly contingent; they will change over time and according to context. However, most of us will have a preponderant style or styles and will avoid others. Thus if we find ourselves in situations in which the prevailing mode is a style that we are not comfortable with, then we are less likely to be engaged and so to learn effectively.

A diagnosis of preferred learning styles can help a learner in a number of ways:

- identification of optimum learning circumstances;
- avoidance of inappropriate learning situations;
- development of alternative strategies;
- relating a learning need to a learning style.

There are also significant implications for teachers because, just as individuals have a preferred learning style, so teachers may well teach in a particular way, possibly quite unconsciously. Without a learning-style diagnosis, there is bound to be a mismatch between the prevailing strategies in the classroom and the preferred styles of its inhabitants. The variation in learning styles might help to explain the often apparently bizarre changes in the degree of involvement on the part of pupils. An inappropriate activity may well produce dysfunctional behaviour. Galton and Simon (1980) identified four types of learner:

- attention seekers;
- intermittent workers;
- solitary workers;
- quiet collaborators.

Every teacher will recognise the types and be aware that the numbers in any one category will vary according to the teaching style in use. It may well be that Galton and Simon have identified the behaviours resulting from the use of inappropriate learning styles.

The capacity to learn is often the result of an interpretive relationship between teacher and learner. The success of that relationship is contingent on the extent to which there are shared constructs. Understanding of learning styles may well be a substantial contribution to optimising the possibility of an effective learning relationship. It is interesting to observe how in classrooms, if given a free choice, children will naturally gravitate to those with whom they can work in harmony. This tendency might be explained by learning styles. What is urgently needed is a range of diagnostic tools which can help to identify learning styles at various stages of children's development.

Teaching strategies

Few topics are as emotive as what constitutes appropriate behaviour by teachers and what are the most effective strategies to facilitate learning. In the case of 'progressive' versus 'traditional' methods, the jury is still out and likely to remain so for the foreseeable future. Indeed it may well be time to call for a mistrial as the charge is misconceived, and misconceived on three grounds. First, the desire to dichotomise is a mark of the modernist, the bureaucrat, for whom neatness of categorisation is more important that attempting to cope with the infinite plurality that is the essence of the learning–teaching process. Second, and related to the first, the division into two neat, polarised approaches, rarely found in their purest forms, is a reflection of the centralist tendency to believe that one can specify teaching styles in total absence of any knowledge of the individual children involved. Finally, the emphasis on the importance of teaching strategies is to give one variable, albeit a highly signifi-cant one, undue prominence and significance. Teaching which is contextual-ised only in terms of the activity of the teacher is going to produce a partial picture. Instead, teaching has to be conceptualised in terms of its relationship to profound learning.

Bennett's (1976) seminal work in describing the spectrum of learning methods provides a helpful classification of patterns of classroom organisation from, on the one hand, a considerable degree of pupil freedom to, on the other, a strong manifestation of teacher control:

- integration of subject matter, pupil choice of work and where to sit, little control of movement, limited testing;
- integrated approach to subjects, low teacher profile, more direction of tasks, pupil choice of seating and movement, limited testing;
- class teaching and group work both used, integrated approach to subjects;
- separate subjects taught but with a high level of pupil choice within the subject areas;
- separate subjects taught through whole-class strategies, limited choice and movement, sanctions employed;
- high emphasis on formal methods and control, together with strong emphasis on assessment.

Bennett's findings, that basic skills among pupils improved in more formal settings, and that more informal classrooms did not raise creativity but could increase anxiety, posed a number of questions that still need to be answered. The point is made that skilled and experienced teachers use a portfolio of strategies. The issue is the basis upon which they make the selection and what range of approaches they are habitually able to employ effectively. Crucially, there needs to be, in the mind of the teacher, a very clear correlation among four elements: the learning strategies that the teacher is enabling the children to employ, the topic under consideration, the needs of the individuals in the class and the types of assessment being used.

What is needed is much more classroom-based research to help create a more sophisticated understanding of the interaction between teaching strategies and the learning of the individual. However, the a priori has to be a definition of learning rather than the assumption that an active teacher automatically equates with internalisation, with deep learning as described in Chapter 4. Such research needs to focus in particular on the basis for the teacher's selection of particular strategies. According to Entwhistle (1988):

> There is some evidence that teaching style is one facet of a general view about the purposes of education. Formal teachers see their role in terms of the narrow view of education in which examination results and vocational training are dominant. Informal teachers stress the pupils' enjoyment of school and opportunities for self-expression. (p238)

Significantly, neither view starts from the basis of how children learn – the factors governing teaching strategies are ideological or based on how the teacher teaches, but not on any view of the processes which might facilitate learning.

Two approaches to teaching as facilitating learning based on explicit principles are the Steiner philosophy and High Scope. In the Steiner approach, the culture in the classroom is very much that of a family with teachers as parents 'working' *with* children, the emphasis being on real tasks interwoven with shared discussion. High Scope also requires high levels of discussion based on the principle of 'plan, do, review'. In both cases, children choose an activity following discussion. In the High Scope approach, the end of an activity involves a period of review which leads to progress being recorded.

Both these approaches involve a very different perception of the role of the teacher from that which is often found; there is a high level of respect for even the youngest child as an individual learner and emphasis on the wide range of activities that have learning potential. High Scope has a proven record in the USA (where it originated) and Britain in significantly raising achievement. What is significant about both approaches is that an understanding of how children learn is translated into specific techniques which are consistently applied.

Cognitive skills

The cognitive aspect of learning is one of the most misunderstood and neglected aspects of the curriculum. The root of the problem is the belief that the 'intellectual demand of the curriculum' has to be matched to the 'current stage of development of the learner'. As Adey and Shayer (1994) state:

A deliberate policy of challenging learners to transcend their present level of thinking not only accelerates their rate of intellectual development, but also in the long-term brings about the achievement which a matching policy on its own would have denied them. (p7)

The deployment of cognitive skills is essentially about teaching thinking, the deliberate, explicit and systematic introduction and use of what might be called higher-order skills – the skills that are common to all intellectual activity but are usually seen as being implicit. Fisher (1990, ppix–x) identifies a number of misconceptions about thinking:

1 Thinking or reasoning is just the fourth 'R'. In fact, he argues, it is the 'foundation skill of all learning'.
2 Reasoning skills are natural functions that improve with age and experience. In fact the skills are the same; it is their application that changes.
3 The teaching of reasoning denies the emotional side of life. In fact, it is the 'linking of reasoning with emotions that provides the prime motivation for learning'.

What is lacking in most education systems is a thinking curriculum to be placed alongside the knowledge curriculum, but working in and through it. There is very powerful evidence that the introduction of the teaching of thinking significantly enhances the performance of children measured by a wide range of outcomes. For example, the use of the CASE approach (Cognitive Acceleration through Science Education) (Adey and Shayer, 1994) led to 42 per cent of boys achieving a grade C or better at GCSE; less than 13 per cent of the control group reached this level. The impact on mathematics and English results was equally dramatic. There is no doubt that this explicit concentration on thinking is vitally important for pupils and for schools wishing to see their pupils do as well as they possibly can.

Of greater significance is the fact that the thinking and the reasoning skills developed through cognitive approaches are what young people need to survive and flourish in a rapidly changing world. The increasing access to information together with its constant growth require the ability to sort, process and use it rather than an increasingly redundant and erroneous memorisation of an externally imposed and narrow 'body of knowledge'.

A key variable in helping children to succeed is the extent to which they have access to the meta-skills. These can be taught, as Fisher and others so powerfully demonstrate. The issue is to make them a significant component of each individual's profile so that they have the requisite skills and techniques available to help them to learn.

A major constraint on this approach is the fact that most teachers and managers in schools have been educated in a culture that did not recognise the significance or validity of cognitive development. Therefore, these are 'new' approaches which are not built into thinking about lesson planning, and are certainly not to the forefront of thinking about management processes.

These cognitive skills, and thus the basis for the thinking curriculum for both pupils and adults, can be summarised as:

- problem-solving;
- critical thinking;
- reasoning;
- creative thinking.

More specific strategies might include:

- recognition and clarification of a problem;
- mapping and ordering relevant information;
- generating alternative solutions;
- applying logical criteria;
- implementing a solution;
- monitoring;
- communicating;
- evaluating outcomes;

- generating conclusions;
- transfer to other situations.

The modules in the Somerset Thinking Skills course provide a most useful starting point for any cognitive development programme:

1 Foundations for problem-solving.

2 Analysing and synthesising.

3 Positioning in time and space.

4 Comparative thinking.

5 Understanding analogies.

6 Patterns in time and space.

7 Organising and memorising.

8 Predicting and deciding.

There are numerous vehicles available to support the introduction of a cognitive approach – see Fisher (1990, 1995) and Coles and Robinson (1991). One particularly significant area of development has been in the introduction of the teaching of logic and philosophy. The Philosophical Inquiry Project at Glasgow University has had a significant impact on primary education. McGavin (1996) reports a teacher's comments about the impact of the project on pupils with emotional and behavioural problems:

> It liberates them from their anger. They have poor literacy skills but they can think perfectly well. Thinking precedes literacy and numeracy, but nowhere in the curriculum is that recognised.

Social skills and behaviour

In the same way that cognitive skills are essential tools for thinking and learning, so social skills are equally significant. Just as the ability to think is a necessary prerequisite, so social skills are an essential component to creating learning schools – partly to facilitate the learning process, but chiefly to ensure that the whole child is educated.

The work of Vygotsky and Feuerstein points to the importance of interpersonal relationships as precursors to effective learning. Vygotsky (1978) argues that learning, the creation of meaning, for the individual develops out of social experiences, especially in language, and is then internalised and made private; this understanding of the world is extended by working with others. Bruner (1996) puts this view very clearly: 'I have come increasingly to recognise that most learning in most settings is a communal activity, a sharing of culture.' Feuerstein seeks to redress physiological and psychological disadvantages through the mediating role of the teacher using specific techniques to enhance the quality of interaction.

It is relatively easy to formulate a list of appropriate and desirable behaviours that exist in any effective group:

- empathetic listening;
- supporting and building;
- recognising and respecting other people's time and space;
- positive reinforcement.

Taken together, these qualities form the basis of most effective social relationships. They are also, of course, what Howard Gardner (1995) calls 'interpersonal intelligence', an intelligence that schools need to foster. Indeed, most of these prevail in most classrooms and staff rooms for most of the time. However, as with thinking skills, there is a very strong case for not leaving these essentials to chance, nor hoping that they will emerge as the result of prescriptions and sanctions, but rather seeking to making them explicit and thereby become the norm. Collins (1996) in her work on the 'quiet child' has identified a range of strategies for enhancing the integration into lessons of children who are shy and withdrawn. In doing so, she has created a vital model for a learning situation based on sophisticated social relationships:

- emphasising the value of talk, and making it the medium for learning rather than the precursor to the 'real' work of writing;
- rejecting whole-class teacher-directed talk in favour of small-group child-centred talk;
- identifying the rules of discussion and making them explicit to pupils;
- increasing feelings of security by establishing friendship groups or 'talk partners' and using them as the basis for all initial discussions;
- providing activities which encourage collaboration;
- giving pupils time to consider what they say before calling them to speak in front of large groups;
- working with pupils to devise ways of assessing talk and what makes for effective talk.

The power of effective social relationships as the basis for learning has been recognised by Taylor and McKenzie (1997) in their work in introducing a team-based culture in classrooms:

> The students of Endeavour Hills have a team book in which they may write about their experiences in their teams. These reflections may be about the actual work, or comments passed on their feelings about their team or themselves. In these books are also the roles that the teams themselves have decided upon and the consequences for breaking those rules ... This is real evidence that these students are taking more responsibility for their own learning and are indeed becoming 'professional learners'. (p158)

What is significant about the approaches of Collins and of Taylor and McKenzie is that they are all advocating specific strategies which seek to create an appropriate environment for learning, rather than a negative culture based on control and sanctions. What they describe and advocate are essentially mature social relationships and it is recognised that different strategies may be needed to move from immature to mature classrooms.

Assertive Discipline

Assertive Discipline (Canter and Canter, 1976) is a classic example of a strategy designed to facilitate the shift from control to assent. Assertive Discipline is posited on two fundamental principles:

1 Explicit and unequivocal negotiated definitions of what constitutes inappropriate behaviour and the consistent application of appropriate sanctions;

2 Positive reinforcement of desired behaviour through the use of praise and rewards.

Anecdotal evidence indicates that Assertive Discipline can have a profound impact on behaviour in a school, significantly reducing the number of 'incidents', increasing the confidence of teachers to deal with issues themselves, and helping to create an hegemony of appropriate behaviour.

Assertive Discipline is a whole-school and whole-class strategy. In the final analysis it works by securing agreement to a code of behaviour through teacher and peer pressure. This agreement, and the method of achieving it, can provide an important step towards social maturity in the schools. It is also a small example of the 'interpretive community', discussed in Chapter 7. Behaviour, instead of being ordained by fiat from the top of a hierarchy, becomes an openly discussed system that enables everyone the more easily to live together in equity.

However, behaviour is learnt, and learnt in a social setting, and the principles of learning appropriate behaviour are the same as those for any piece of knowledge or set of skills. The basis has to be the understanding of and the internalisation by the individual. Thus Feverstein's notion of mediation seems to provide the most fitting model.

Mentoring and coaching

Success in learning is as much contingent upon how one learns as it is on what one learns. We have argued that learning is a highly subjective process; however, this does not preclude the possibility of mediation and intervention. Mentoring is emerging as one of the most powerful forms of intervention; if it is combined with the principles of coaching then the following components emerge:

- a one-to-one relationship;
- regular and formalised meetings;
- negotiated agendas led by the learner;
- systematic diagnosis and analysis;
- target setting;
- review and reinforcement.

The essential element of the relationship is the detailed and systematic feedback on performance and the identification of appropriate strategies to improve that performance against mutually agreed targets. The parallels with coaching for improving performance in a sports setting are precise.

In the context of learning, the coach has to work with the individual. It is impossible to coach a whole class except in the most rudimentary basic skills; once they are established, then the strategies have to be bespoke – appropriate to the individual at a given and understood stage of development. The relationship has to be based on a high degree of mutual trust and respect (and is in turn likely to deepen both), and the primary responsibility of the mentor/coach has to be to create opportunities for success.

Aspects of this relationship are, of course, already found in most schools, though often confined to the gym and the sports field. Most reading schemes based on an interventionist approach require one-to-one relationships. The most successful work with children with emotional or behavioural difficulties is on an individual basis. Many schools have found that coaching is the most powerful way to improve performance in public examinations; groups that have had mentoring built into the working pattern outperform groups that have not. The power of this mode of working is perhaps best exemplified in two extremes: the parent helping the young child to walk, talk, wash and so on, and the university tutor working with a student in the classic tutorial. In both cases, there is a relationship that transcends teacher and taught. It might be worth drawing a distinction between coaching as a process to develop specific skills and abilities and mentoring as a more holistic process responsible for the evolution of the individual learner. As such there are many potential coaches in a school, almost every pupil having the potential to coach another in some aspect of the curriculum. Peer tutoring has the advantages of being immediate, less threatening and more specifically focused on actual needs and strategies that work. Coaches and mentors might be peers; they can also be drawn from a wide range of sources:

- the fit, active widow of 74 who dotes on her grandchildren, spends most of her time alone and who, for the cost of a taxi-fare, could spend, say, ten hours a week listening to children read;

- the staff of a firm each giving 30 minutes a week to their local primary school;
- the redundant craftsman supporting technology projects;
- the early-retired office manager providing support for IT skills.

Thus a 15-year-old could experience coaching and mentoring in a wide variety of ways:

- providing support for a reading programme in a local primary school;
- being coached by a sixth-former in the more esoteric mysteries of algebra;
- being mentor to a Year 7 learning team;
- being mentored by a full-time member of the teaching staff in preparation for 16+ examinations;
- being coached in learning to play the cello.

This example is unlikely to work in totality within the confines of the present secondary school day. Aspects of it are found in the primary school and it is a distinctive feature of best practice in further and higher education. It would require a significant realignment of the deployment of time in many secondary schools to create a coaching and mentoring culture.

As with many other aspects of effective learning, changes in the way that adults work in schools may be a necessary prerequisite to changing the way that young people learn.

Joyce and Showers (1980) argued that training for development is made up of five elements:

- presentation of theory;
- demonstration or modelling;
- practice;
- feedback on performance;
- coaching.

Joyce and Showers claim that teachers who have been coached display the following characteristics:

- changes in behaviour were much more likely to occur;
- knowledge of new techniques was likely to be retained for longer;
- greater understanding was achieved of the purposes and uses of strategies.

Most teachers on courses (and most pupils in schools) experience the first four elements listed above with varying degrees of effectiveness. Comparatively few experience the fifth dimension, ie the stage which facilitates understanding and application, the stage which increases the possibility of real learning taking place.

Feedback, recognition and reinforcement

Learning in schools takes place within a social context, and the success of the individual learner will be significantly determined by the perceived validity of social relationships. The extent to which individuals feel valued, respected and reinforced will be a major factor in consolidating their capacity to learn. Social relationships are a major determinant of self-perception and so of self-esteem and motivation. The extent to which schools can be socially sophisticated institutions remains problematic. At the most fundamental level, there is a question mark over how far the very organisational patterns of schools allow for the development of effective relationships.

Keys and Fernandes (1993) in their report 'What do students think about their school?' found that 40 per cent of secondary pupils go for a year without discussing a single piece of their work with teachers. Only 6 or 7 per cent had discussed their work 'often'. Such a situation makes it almost impossible to generate the communication and positive feedback essential to motivation and the creation of a positive attitude. This research was based on the secondary school as was the work by Barber and Graham (1994), who investigated the decline in motivation after Year 7:

> When asked why there was a dramatic fall in enthusiasm, the reply from groups of Year 9 and 10 pupils was that the school had looked after them well and carefully in Year 7; success had come reasonably readily and had always been recognised and commended.

> In Year 8 the work got harder and ... the teachers became much less overtly supportive.

This process was compounded in Years 9 and 10, and resulted in an inevitable fall in morale and performance and a rise in behavioural problems. Barber and Graham found that the transition from a primary school culture to the ways of working in the secondary school was a major factor in determining future success. They noted that schools had introduced a number of strategies to redress the decline:

1 effective differentiation so that all children are given tasks suited to their capabilities;
2 high investment in tutorial work to encourage a focus on the individual;
3 high emphasis on out-of-school activities to enhance social relationships and increase the mutual understanding between teacher and pupil.

Harris and Russ (1994) found that in a study of eight inner-city schools which had raised pupil achievement

> learning seemed to improve if pupils were given precise feedback on their progress in each subject area through written or verbal comment so that they knew what they needed to do better and how to do it.

Learning was also strengthened where efforts were made to involve all pupils and where teachers encouraged pupils to work together to develop their own self-esteem.

Many children regularly experience positive feedback and praise and have high self-esteem. However, if a school is to be confident of enhancing the learning of every individual, then it has to reduce the variation between teachers and classrooms. A culture has to be created based on strategies that facilitate achievement. One of the ways in which such a culture can be established is for the adults in the school frequently to be seen at work by team leaders and the headteacher and deputy headteachers, and encouraged, praised, mentored and helped to develop. Indeed, it is difficult to envision a school in which pupils are consistently individually encouraged and helped, but in which adults work for the majority of the time in isolation and unappreciated.

According to Barnard (*TES*, 22 March 1996, p4), achievement can be improved through 'Habits of the Mind':

1 setting long- and short-term goals;

2 learning to manage time to complete tasks;

3 linking effort to results;

4 creating an optimistic outlook;

5 reflective problem-solving;

6 tolerance of limits and rules set by the school;

7 high frustration tolerance;

8 tolerance of others;

9 independence, self-belief and self-motivation;

10 risk-taking.

Children are the first to recognise, and disregard, spurious or gratuitous praise. Barnard's approach allows for the possibility of increased achievement and so the praise will be seen by the child as being valid, and the recognition and reinforcement will help foster a keener enthusiasm for the learning.

A number of principles can be proposed for appropriate praise-giving:

- It relates to a particular achievement.
- It is personal – specific to an individual.
- It is immediate – instant reinforcement.
- It is specific – the recipient knows exactly what the praise is being given for.
- It consolidates – identifies the appropriate behaviour, skills, etc, and thus helps the recipient repeat the good practice.
- It needs to be openhandedly generous.

Two important points emerge from these principles. First, they do not preclude group celebration of success – the class spending, for example, the final ten minutes of the day celebrating individual and group successes. Secondly, and as with feedback and encouragement, there needs to be a culture in the school in which everyone's achievement is praised and celebrated; we all need far more praise than blame, and praise is more likely to lead to further success.

Multiple intelligences

One of the most significant barriers to learning is an arcane view of what constitutes intelligence. Work in France, the USA and the UK in the first half of the twentieth century created a fallacious orthodoxy about intelligence which still dominates educational policy-making, school organisations and teacher behaviour. The three elements of this fallacy are:

1 Intelligence is fixed at birth.
2 Intelligence is defined only in terms of logical/reasoning ability; it follows, therefore, that a deficiency in such ability implies limited intelligence.
3 Intelligence can be measured through simple testing.

Logic and reasoning assumed pre-eminence because they lent themselves to spurious quantification and thereby classification. This combination was irresistible to generations of educators who were beguiled by the myths of objectivity and stratification. Such an approach helped reinforce prevailing views of what constituted the academic canon and notions of the inevitability and desirability of social class. IQ testing is probably one of the most unjust and iniquitous procedures in education. Most significant is the denial of the full potential of individuals – including those regarded as being 'intelligent' because of the near exclusive emphasis on one aspect of their capacity to learn.

The most significant challenge to the orthodoxy of IQ has been the work of Howard Gardner, and in particular *Frames of Mind*. The impact of his work, and others working in the fields of neurology and cognitive psychology, is to create new principles about the nature of human intelligence and hence the capacity to learn:

- intelligence is not fixed at birth – it can be enhanced by every individual;
- the process of improving intelligence can be taught;
- intelligence is a multiple reality – it can be expressed in many forms;
- acts of the intellect require a range of intelligences to work together in varying proportions according to the task;
- learning requires an understanding of the various intelligences and the ability to relate them to specific activities.

According to Gardner there are seven intelligences:

- *Verbal/linguistic intelligence.* This relates to the use of language and, notably, reasoning, symbolic thinking and the ability to work at a conceptual level.

- *Logical/mathematical intelligence.* This is focused on deductive and inductive reasoning, ie the ability to observe, draw conclusions and develop hypotheses. It is also expressed in the ability to recognise patterns and thus to establish relationships.

- *Visual/spatial intelligence.* This is expressed through the visual arts and spatial activity involving the capacity to think in three dimensions, as, for example, in architecture. Chess is an example of a game involving spatial intelligence.

- *Body/kinesthetic intelligence.* This manifests itself in the use of the body in an expressive mode, such as in dance or in playing games in which a range of sophisticated, coordinated responses are required.

- *Musical/rhythmic intelligence.* This involves the recognition and use of patterns of rhythm and tone found in musical instruments, the voice, nature, etc. In many ways it is the most compelling intelligence making the most immediate impact on the brain.

- *Interpersonal intelligence.* This manifests itself in the ability to interact with, understand and respond to others.

- *Intrapersonal intelligence.* This is concerned with self-knowledge about how we function as a sentient being. It is about awareness of self, self-conceptualisation and the understanding of personal potential.

Gardner has demonstrated that each of these intelligences is directly related to a specific area of the brain. That means that it is a neurological function and can therefore be developed as with any other part of the body. The implications of multiple intelligence theory for learning are profound. As Gardner himself expresses it:

> It's my belief that virtually any topic and any concept can be approached in a number of ways, and that optimal teaching makes it possible for the largest range of students to learn about the range of human knowledge ... Teachers should be able to present materials using several intelligences; and learners – intrapersonally intelligent about themselves should be able to bootstrap themselves to superior understanding in a way most appropriate to their own cognitive profile. (1991, pvi)

The practical implications of an approach to learning based on the theory of multiple intelligences might include:

- the diagnosis of an individual's existing capabilities across the range of multiple intelligences;

- systematic development through specific activities of the intelligences that are relatively weak;

- designing tasks and projects using multiple intelligences as one of the criteria for the learning strategies;

- creating work areas/classrooms that give equal significance to all the intelligences;

- encouraging reflection about learning within the areas of each intelligence;
- ensuring that teacher development incorporates activities in all the intelligences;
- ensuring that the range of modes of assessment parallel the full range of intelligences;
- ensuring that the human, material and time resources of the school are deployed in such a way as to reflect the school's commitment to the development of all the intelligences;
- deploying what Lazear (in Gardner, 1991) describes as a 'Multiple Intelligences Toolbox' – a range of practical activities associated with each intelligence;
- ensuring that the school celebrates each student's growing maturity in and mastery of each intelligence.

Prior knowledge

(This section develops some of the ideas in Chapter 4.)

One of the major barriers to learning for understanding is an information/ content-based grouping of subjects which implicitly defines learning as the demonstrated acquisition of facts rather than showing an understanding of and an ability to use in new areas those facts. There is a deal of bravado shown in schools' publishing schedules of what is to be learnt as such schedules ignore the uncertainties about the nature and status of knowledge. Such 'schemes of work' also underline the transmissive mode of teaching in that they rely on the control structures of schools, such as timetables and chronologically lock-stepped pupils.

Also, as respect for the prior knowledge of children is not implicit in the way that many classrooms work, teachers do not recognise there to be any problem. Gardner (1993) expresses the problem thus:

> *At last we can confront directly the primary reasons why school is difficult. It is difficult, first, because much of the material presented in school strikes many students as alien, if not pointless ... It is difficult, second, because some of these notational systems, concepts and frameworks and epistemic terms are not readily mastered by students whose intellectual strengths may lie in other areas or approaches.* (p149)

Gardner goes on to argue that there may well be a collision between the scholastic terms of knowing and the symbolic knowing developed before school. The result of such a collision can only be a 'scrambling' of understanding with a denial of the personal in favour of the official – what Gardner refers to as 'correct-answer compromises'. Such compromises can only deny learning, because learning in school is not organised in such a way as to mediate with and respond to students' existing interpretations of the world.

No child or student comes to a lesson as a *tabula rasa*. Social and intuitive learning will have created a series of understandings, a reality, which have perfect validity as explanations of the world and what makes it function for that individual. The student comes to the lesson with a created reality. Embarking on a programme of learning without recognising that reality, those prior understandings, may well serve only to confuse and diminish the learner. As Gardner (1991) expresses it:

> *Education for understanding comes about only if students somehow become able to integrate the prescholastic with the scholastic and disciplinary ways of knowing and, when such integration does not prove possible, to suspend or replace the prescholastic ways of knowing in favor of the scholastic forms of knowing. Finally, students need to be able to appreciate when a prescholastic form of knowing may harbour a different or even deeper form of understanding than the discipline related form of knowing learned in school.* (p149)

Gardner goes on to provide numerous examples from the sciences and humanities of what he calls 'misconceptions', 'rigidly applied algorithms', 'stereotypes' and 'simplifications'. He goes to great pains to stress that the use of the these terms does not imply a hierarchy of significance or inadequacy: 'All understandings are partial and subject to change' (p152). Gardner places less emphasis on the status of the 'correct' view than on understanding of the processes involved. He draws a fundamentally important distinction between 'earlier understandings' and 'more elaborated forms of understanding'.

If a key criterion of a successful learning process is the creation of understanding, then that process has to start where the learner is. This is well known in the folklore of teaching, ie 'moving from the known to the unknown'. Unfortunately the known is usually measured in terms of levels of acquisition and success in replication rather than internalised understanding. If learning is to be facilitated, then three factors have to be taken into account:

1   The current modes of understanding of the individual learner, ie a diagnosis of what is understood and how it is expressed. Learning what the current modes of understanding are implies a highly individualised negotiation in order to develop a clear map of where the learner is and, more importantly, how he or she got there.

2   The identification of the appropriate means of conveying meaning and so creating understanding. Those who facilitate learning need to draw on a wide range of forms of knowing: sensorimotor, symbolic, notational, conceptual and epistemic.

3   The development of appropriate processes and relationships between teacher and learner — what Gardner (1993) describes as apprenticeship:

The weaver in a preliterate society just models and adds a few words of explanation; the weaver in a literate society can make use of charts, diagrams, mathematical equations, and books. Unlike the the traditional schoolteacher, however, the weaver who teaches for understanding draws upon these epistemic forms when they arise in the course of a genuine problem, a challenging project, a valuable product. A judicious introduction and integration of apprenticeship methods within a scholastic setting should yield students whose potential of understanding is engaged and enhanced.

There are, of course, a number of implications for schools once teachers accept that 'we start where the learner is'. The most fundamental is, clearly, that the culture of the school will have to change; it will need to change from one in which implicitly and explicitly the main emphasis is on enabling teachers to teach, to one in which the main emphasis is on enabling children to learn. There are many schools which are making this change, and as part of the change are putting in place the 'learning manager' who is responsible for the learning of a group of students. That manager, or tutor, is responsible for seeing that the human and material resources available in the school are deployed in the best possible way to match the learning needs and styles of the individual students. Time has to be given for those managers really to get to know the individuals in the group. Everyone in the school has to accept that paradox which says: 'Less is more.' In other words, the school, through the leadership of the learning managers, accepts the idea of less content and less scampering after the chimera of 'getting through the material', and instead has a clear focus on how to fit new ideas, new maps into the existing reality that the children bring with them. Only by such a shift in focus can schools ensure deep learning.

Health and diet

Mens sana in corpore sano (a sound mind in a healthy body) is one of the lasting clichés, almost banal now in its usage. It is a cliché, of course, because of its essential truth, a truth that is being reasserted by the growing amount of research into the links between our diet and exercise patterns and the sorts of people we are. Every teacher knows that physiological issues have an often disproportionate impact on a child's ability to learn. The young person who is going to learn to optimum effect is probably in a state which can best be described as 'well-being'. The characteristics of this state might be identified as:

- a balanced, nutritious and regular diet;
- adequate sleep and rest;
- regular and appropriate exercise;
- psychological equilibrium;
- appropriate and timely medication and treatment.

Virtually all of these factors are outside the immediate control of the teacher and the school. Children come to school with inadequate sleep, no breakfast, have an unbalanced diet and may often have been disturbed by a range of dysfunctional social experiences. The diet that they do have may well be high in sugar and tartrazine which can result in minor or major changes in the child's behaviour pattern.

As with diet, schools are virtually powerless over social distress. Yet with 24 per cent of children in Britain living at or below the poverty line, there are limited grounds for hoping that the well-being of the children in our schools at the moment will improve in any measurable way before they leave. What is equally clear is that *teaching* about a healthy way of life is not working. Lessons about healthy living in food technology sessions appear to have limited impact once the children reach the school canteen. Sex education as part of the taught curriculum does not work: Britain has the highest rate of teenage pregnancy in Europe. Lessons on the dangers of drugs do not have an effect: young people, some very young people, regularly take drugs as part of their entertainment. Clearly these lessons are examples of one of the major themes of this book – that shallow learning, the taking in and regurgitating of facts, is instantly forgettable; it has no impact on self, and therefore no impact on behaviour. Children can get ten out ten on any number of tests on 'What should you eat to be healthy?', and immediately go out and gorge cheerfully on the junkiest of foods.

Furthermore, schools have a limited capacity to improve the situation in a child's home in which a lone parent has about £20 a week to spend on food. Changes of that sort are not within a school's immediate area of responsibility.

However, schools can begin to help learners understand the factors that contribute to their effectiveness as learners, ie take a holistic view of the person as a learner. People cannot learn if their bodies or their minds are being maltreated, and children need to be helped, in as practical a way as possible, to understand how, for example, a lack of a vitamin has a direct effect on brain activity, how exercise, in stimulating the intake of oxygen, can have an overall effect on body and mind, or how stress by releasing chemicals into the bloodstream can change behaviour.

There are very many studies available which show how diet and learning are linked. For example, Ostrander and Ostrander (1994) devote a whole chapter to the impact of diet on the functioning of the brain. There is much evidence to show that there is a correlation between certain types of foodstuffs and the ability to concentrate, the function of the memory and so on. There are plenty of commonsense examples that do not require esoteric investigations: a child that has had no breakfast does not work well; a staff meeting at the end of the day will not work well if everyone's blood sugar level is low. It may well be that a basic, but far-reaching, innovation that schools can undertake (and indeed very many have undertaken) to improve learning is to provide brown bread and fruit to pupils at the start of the day and to staff before a meeting at the end.

Many schools have sought to provide a more appropriate diet to pupils at lunch time, but probably negate this by selling confectionery and fizzy drinks during the breaks. The problems of an unhealthy diet, and the parallel concerns about childhood (and adult) obesity, are, however, national and not susceptible to being solved solely at school level. It might be possible, nevertheless, for schools to shift the emphasis away from diet as an abstract notion of health to a focus on diet as a means of enhancing learning and so educational performance. A GCSE or 'A' level revision programme might include advice about diet as a precursor to the usual information about revision techniques. Sports coaching might be used as an exemplar.

Schools might also consider more long-term ways of helping children and their parents to achieve better diets. Many writers have emphasised the need for the boundaries between schools and their communities to become permeable, the argument being in part that schools on their own cannot do all that children need, and in part that if we are to break down the notion that education and schooling are not to be seen as the same thing then school and community need to overlap at as many points as possible. Community-based courses, set up and run on a multi-agency basis using the school's premises and personnel, could begin to look at, for example, what is meant by 'healthy eating', what sorts of cooking are best in that community, how budgets might be best used, how groups can get together to bulk-buy thus helping to reduce costs, how and what sorts of exercise can help.

There is a logic in such a suggestion. We have stressed many times in this book that the core purpose of schools is to enable all in them to learn. If a major block is discovered which makes learning more difficult, or even impossible, then the school has a duty to look to every means to try to remove it. The block may be internal – the vagaries of the average school timetable. It may be external – the diet of many people in its community. In either case, the school needs to look for a solution, either on its own or alongside the community which it serves.

What is being suggested is that in this area, as in so many others, the neat boundaries, the boxes beloved of bureaucracies, can militate against what schools need and want to do. It cannot be said that such and such an area is 'the curriculum' and such and such an area is that person's poor diet. At the centre is the child's learning: it may be that a child cannot learn because of poor hearing, or another finds it difficult to read because of poor eyesight, or another is withdrawn because of a speech impediment, or that some children cannot pay attention because their diet contributes to their excessive activity. In each case the teacher needs to diagnose the cause of the problem and then get the help that is needed to remediate it.

The person is not cured by having a symptom eliminated; the child cannot learn if the root cause of the problem is left undisturbed. The 'learning manager' mentioned above has the task to see the children in his or her group holistically, and to seek ways to take away the barriers to their learning. The suggestion put forward here is that schools and the community together might seek for some imaginative solutions to problems which the school on its own cannot hope to find.

Intrinsic motivation

One of the great fallacies about teaching and managing is that it is possible for one person to motivate another (or even more absurdly for one person to motivate a large group, ie a class). Motivation is a highly subjective phenomenon and the motivation to learn, in particular, is not amenable to external threats or promises. These can result in a temporary change in superficial behaviour but will not alter fundamental attitudes. It is easy to prove this point by looking at the list of those students who appear for detention; the same pupils appear time after time, demonstrating that threats and actual punishment have little if any effect. Unless the individual accepts and internalises the need to change or engage in a change in fundamental attitude the response will always be superficial and transitory.

In essence, intrinsic motivation is an individual psychological contract in which the outcome is seen as being valid and significant and there is a high probability that the expenditure of energy will actually lead to its achievement. Thus the learner has to accept the desirability of an activity in personal terms and believe that it is not only worth achieving but that the ratio of commitment to success is very high.

Classic motivation theory

Classic motivation theory (eg Maslow and Herzberg) works on the basis of a hierarchy of significance. However, contemporary thinking would indicate that this hierarchy has to be understood in individual terms. We (the authors) cannot anticipate your motives for reading this book. It might be for the joy of intellectual debate, professional enrichment and personal growth. It might be that you have an MA assignment to complete and this book is the quickest way into the topic. It may just be that this is the only thing available to read and it is better to read this than to sit gazing into space. (Whatever your motivation we hope that the commitment results in satisfaction.)

If individuals are to be motivated to learn then a number of practical steps would seem to be appropriate:

1 a high degree of knowledge about the learner, the learner's values, priorities, hopes, needs and expectations;

2 a sophisticated diagnosis of the existing level of skill and knowledge to ensure that outcomes, while challenging, are possible and attainable;

3 abundant opportunities for success – motivation is a correlation of success more than failure;

4 the identification of targets which are meaningful to the learner;

5 regular feedback, reinforcement, recognition and praise;

6 ensuring that the learner has the resources to be able to complete the task;

7 ensuring that the learner accepts the validity of the activity in personal terms;

8 regular monitoring to ensure that the activity retains its motivational force. This last item may be the point at which the cycle restarts, as the loss of motivation can mean the cessation of learning, and so the coach/mentor would go back to points 1, 2 and/or 3 to see what had changed and what needed to be done to help the learner.

Two factors are common to these points, and to others raised elsewhere in this and other chapters. The first is the idea of the coach/mentor or learning manager, establishing the relationship with the learner necessary to create understanding and negotiate meaning. Second there is the need to organise work into coherent tasks, linked to targets, which makes it understandable and attainable on the individual's terms.

Intrinsic motivation is an important factor in developing autonomous learners. Inspiration is another such factor. It is interesting to look at the difference between the two. The former is the more direct, the more pointed – motivation is defined as 'the providing of an incentive'. It is within the competencies needed by a coach or mentor to be able to help learners in his or her care to become self-motivated in the way described above. On the other hand, inspiration is the more indirect and might be said to infuse an institution or a group. Any leader needs to be able to inspire; there is a spiritual quality about the idea of inspiration, and it is sometimes difficult, if not impossible, to state exactly what action or word or behaviour is the cause of the inspiration. One definition is 'unacknowledged prompting'. Motivation is to management as inspiration is to leadership.

Access to resources

An alternative title to this section might be the 'geography of learning'. We have argued that learning is an individual phenomenon. It therefore follows that the individual has to be able to control access to the resources necessary to facilitate learning. In this context, resources can be categorised in the following way:

- teachers and other adults;
- other learners;
- skills;
- sources of information (libraries, computer programs, Internet);
- hardware (computers, learning materials, audiovisual equipment).

The fundamental principle is that the autonomous learner has to have access to a wide range of appropriate resources, together with the skills to make the best use of them, on his or her own terms. Control by the teachers or other adults in the school or college of resources reinforces the notion of dependency; it is as if the learner has to ask permission to learn. A powerful example of how this approach might work is provided by Trott (1997):

> *The Mereway Middle School Challenge Centre is a multi-purpose facility. It is equipped with up-to-date multimedia technology and communications systems for the children's use. To date these include computers with CD-ROM, lap-tops, a modem, telephone, fax, Internet connection, cameras, video player and video camera.*
>
> *The work of the Challenge Centre has three main loci:*
>
> *It provides us with an attractive, well resourced space which can be used by children, and staff supporting children ...*
>
> *The Challenge Centre provides us with a supplementary facility for advanced IT work with children and IT training for staff.*
>
> *It provides a focus for 'Challenges' which are introduced to the children from a variety of sources ... Challenges are often tailor-made for the children and relate to real problems or projects. As a consequence of this, children are usually able to see some of their ideas and solutions put into action.* (pp182–3)

Two factors militate against the approach described by Trott. First, there is the historic perception by some teachers of their role as controller and dispenser. Second, there is the major problem of the geography of most schools which serves to isolate teachers and classes. Practice in many primary and middle schools demonstrates that it is possible to break out of the psychological constraint of the four walls. At the very least it is possible to think of classrooms as each being a 'challenge centre'. If individual timetables are in use, then classrooms become different types of learning centres. They can be:

- computer labs;
- teamworking areas;
- individual reading and study areas;
- whole-class teaching areas;
- teleconferencing centres;
- spaces for coaching and mentoring.

Provision of resources is inevitably constrained by financial considerations. However, we would argue that a flexible access approach offers the opportunity for a more cost-effective utilisation of existing resources. Equally, a decision to focus on learning will have significant medium- and short-term implications for budgeting priorities.

Neurological factors

It is perhaps bizarre, but unsurprising, that those ostensibly concerned with learning have a limited understanding of the processes by which learning takes place, ie brain processes. Perkins (1992) argues that 'learning is a consequence of thinking' (p78), and to this can be added that thinking is a product of neurological processes. Because knowledge of brain functioning has been so limited until now, educationalists have looked to the social sciences to describe and explain the learning process – it is now becoming increasingly possible to understand the process in terms of neurological activity.

Capra (1996) makes the relationship between mind and brain quite clear:

> *Mind is not a thing but a process – the process of cognition, which is identified with the process of life. The brain is a specific structure through which this process operates. The relationship between mind and brain, therefore, is one between process and structure.* (p171)

If learning is about cognition, then the knowledge that is necessary to facilitate it is knowledge about how the brain works. Caine and Caine (1997) argue for the following principles of what they describe as brain/mind learning:

- The brain is a complex dynamic system.
- The brain is a social brain.
- The search for meaning is innate.
- The search for meaning occurs through 'patterning'.
- Emotions are critical to patterning.
- Every brain simultaneously perceives and creates parts and wholes.
- Learning involves both focused attention and peripheral perception.
- Learning always involves conscious and unconscious processes.
- We have at least two ways of organising memory.
- Learning is developmental.
- Complex learning is enhanced by challenge and inhibited by threat.
- Every brain is uniquely organised.

According to Caine (1997):

We have to address how our own brains learn – and immerse ourselves in interactive, real life, complex experiences out of which we can process new ideas.

Brain learning challenges historical models of learning and many orthodoxies surrounding learning. The important information that teachers will need in the future will be biologically rather than sociologically derived. One practical example of a learning strategy which is directly derived from an understanding of how the brain processes information is the notion of neural branching (Cordellichio and Field, 1997). When faced with a wide range of complex stimuli, the brain engages in a process of 'neural pruning', ie it selects and prioritises key data. This process means that we can survive in a complex and stimulating world. However, this pruning process inhibits our ability to perceive information. Many teaching and learning strategies encourage neural pruning and so limit the potential for learning. Neural branching (the opposite of neural pruning) is considered desirable because:

Current research indicates that this type of significant 'brain work' strengthens the brain – creating more synapses between nerve cells – just as exercise builds muscle tissue. (p33)

Cordellichio and Field (1997) propose seven strategies to exercise the brain:

1 *Hypothetical thinking* – this forces learners to conceive of issues and consequences other than the standard and expected ones.

2 *Reversal* – a specific kind of hypothetical thinking that highlights attributes of events or situations that might otherwise go unnoticed.

3 *Applications of different symbol systems* – eg exchanging the verbal and numerical symbol systems.

4 *Analogy* – looking for correspondences.

5 *Analysis of point of view* – understanding why a body of opinion is help by another person.

6 *Completion* – providing alternative conclusions to stories – for example, to illustrate the possibility of multiple responses and the importance of logical inference.

7 *Web analysis* – establishing causal relationships.

There is nothing new in these strategies; what is different is that they are offered as part of a systematic approach to enhancing thinking capacity and so learning. Greater emphasis on neural development through the use of activities designed to stimulate the brain would appear to be a fundamental prerequisite for effective learning. It may well be that Mental Education requires the same emphasis in the curriculum as Physical Education.

Information technology

Throughout this book, there has been a theme running, implicitly or explicitly, that IT is the single most powerful change creator in the history of humankind. One of the major problems that schools face is that they are increasingly asynchronous with the world from which their children and parents come. In part the problem is created by the teaching profession itself; there has been a reluctance to accept the changes that IT creates. In the main, however, the problem has been created by an unwillingness to provide schools with the changed architecture and resources that a proper and wide-ranging use of IT demands.

This section is a brief summary of the main points relating to the place and uses of IT in schools and colleges. There are three main areas of use:

1 the organisation and presentation of information – eg word processing, spreadsheets, databases, spellchecks;

2 programs which facilitate processing information – eg learning packages such as ILS, Successmaker, Plato;

3 access to information – eg CD-ROMs, Internet sites.

What these offer is:

● information on the learner's terms (not the teacher's);

● individualised access and control;

● structured progression at the user's own pace;

● ability to repeat;

● the possibility of error-free work;

● individual interaction;

● absence of problems in that interaction (personality clashes are minimised);

● the ability for the individual to work alone or with a small group;

● enhancement of creativity;

● learning free of time limitation;

● learning free of geographical limitations;

● learning free from assumptions about limitations.

In very brief terms – the learner is in control. It is perhaps that statement that most surely sums up both the excitement and the fears that surround IT.

Examples now abound of schools which have accepted the advent of IT and put it to use. We offer just one. Dettman (1997) describes the scene in the Methodist Ladies College in Melbourne:

A visitor now would see every girl aged 10 and above using her own portable computer for most of the day. The young learners might be using MicroWorlds to construct a detailed map of Australia by plotting co-ordinates or to design a walk tour of their local district, highlighting places of interest. Others might be working with LegoDacta to create sophisticated models controlled by input and output sensors linked by the laptop. Others would be downloading information from Internet or CD ROM without having to leave their desks. A multimedia group would have students recording field trip experiences with scanners and digitising equipment.

IT changes – changes the way we do things, our expectations, our preconceptions about children's limitations, our relationships with our students; it changes the boundaries of time and place within which we have always had to work; it opens up connections impossible only ten years ago. Every week, in journal after journal, there are examples of the imaginative and creative ways in which IT is being used to help children learn more, more easily, more rapidly, more pleasantly. All schools now need to learn from the many that have taken on IT, and put it at the heart of children's learning.

Conclusion

This chapter has looked at a number of ways in which children learn. Each has been dealt with comparatively briefly, either because the topic is dealt with elsewhere in the book or because it is a topic that could take up a chapter in its own right. Taken as a whole, this chapter could form the basis for the description of the tasks to be undertaken by a learning manager. As schools focus increasingly on the management of learning so the present structures will need to alter. There will be a decreasing need for the present pyramid structure which is in place mainly for the organisation of adults. Instead, there will be a need for a more horizontal structure, one which replicates the way the individual child encounters his or her experience of school. The prime responsibility of the learning manager will be – indeed *is* in those schools in which such a structure is already in place – to get to know the individual child as well as possible, and then to ensure that a minimum of barriers hinder that child's learning. The task will be to ensure that the curriculum and the means by which the child experiences the curriculum do not become a procrustean bed.

6
■ ■ ■

Leadership for Learning

Leadership for meaning, leadership for problem solving, collegial leadership, leadership as shared responsibility, leadership that serves school purposes, leadership that is tough enough to demand a great deal from everyone, and leadership that is tender enough to encourage the heart – these are the images of leadership we need for schools as communities. (T. J. Sergiovanni, *Leadership for the Schoolhouse*)

This chapter has two main aims. The first is to examine the language which is used to talk about leadership in schools to see how far that language is compatible with the idea, central to this book, that learning is the core purpose of schools. The second is to suggest that an alternative language is needed, and to look at the changes in leadership that the alternative language will bring about.

The vocabulary of leadership

Leadership has accrued to itself a particular vocabulary over the years, and this vocabulary carries with it not only surface meanings but also, and perhaps more importantly, perceptions, expectations and behaviour. In other words, leadership is not merely a set of skills or qualities, which the surface vocabulary points to, but is also an attitude which informs behaviour. There are, as Sergiovanni (1992) wrote in his book *Moral Leadership*, 'theories of practice' which leaders develop over time, and these theories act as the sounding board which leaders use to test their reactions to the situations that they meet.

Attitudes and 'theories of practice' are constructs derived from the prevailing culture and expressed, reinforced and elaborated into practice through language. The vocabulary, the working definitions and above all the metaphors surrounding and illuminating leadership are powerful forces in formulating attitudes. All these linguistic expressions of leadership are continually reinforced through what is encountered on a day-to-day basis in schools – for example, the symbolism of schools, the content of development and training activities, and the discourse that is employed in all those events. This common language is essentially the culture of the school.

If schools are to respond to the fundamental changes that are taking place in the world that our children will be inhabiting, then it is vital to reconceptualise leadership. In British society in particular, much of the formulation of the concept of leadership is essentially nineteenth century in origin. At the base of this concept is the notion that the British are subjects and not citizens, and this fundamental way of looking at the place of the individual in society has had a profound impact on how the language of leadership has developed and the way in which the practice based on that language has been accepted. In essence, leadership is expressed in terms of individuality and hierarchy, and in an essentially masculine language.

This way of thinking about leadership has produced a culture of formal accountability, control and dependency. However much this culture is mitigated by personal characteristics, the fact remains that most schools are essentially archaic in organisational terms, resembling classic bureaucracies which, by definition, lack the flexibility and adaptability needed at this time. More importantly, the fixed bureaucracy is built to withstand change, and does not respond to demands for transformation, indeed is antithetical to it.

Leadership and transformation

If a school, or any other organisation, is to be capable of being transformed, then it has to be led by people who are capable of personal transformation. By 'transformation' is meant undergoing a cultural change, a change in which the most fundamental aspects of the organisation alter and regrow. Again and again in this book, the need for such fundamental change is stressed as being the only way in which our schools can meet the needs of the children who will be living in the next millennium. If schools are to be able to change in such a way, if they are to re-engineer themselves, then one of the starting points has to be the re-engineering of the perceptions of leadership.

We all have a map, a mindscape, of what we mean by leadership, and one of the main determinants of this map is experience. The experience that we, as children and teachers, have of leadership in schools is expressed through a number of key concepts:

*Head*teacher

Senior management team

Line management

117

Head of department

Examinations *officer*

etc.

Although the practice can and does vary, the underlying mindset is one of hierarchy, control and linearity. Somewhat paradoxically, this language is combined with that of professionalism. In the drive to improve schools (and that term will for the moment be allowed to pass unquestioned), more and more reliance has been put on 'efficient management' and indeed the words 'professionalism' and 'efficiency' are seen by many to be twin aspects of the good leader. One of the aspects of this 'efficiency' is a belief that there are right answers to every problem, and that these right answers can be produced only by 'professionals'. Since the Enlightenment there has been the belief in the 'scientific' method, the belief that says that as long as one approaches a problem in a scientific way, breaks the whole into parts to see what makes it (the problem being addressed) work, then a solution will be found. Imagination, creativity or artistic insight have little part to play. Our current picture of a 'leader' is of a person who has the skill to solve problems by clear, 'objective' thought and application of 'scientifically' validated answers. Moreover, the idea of 'leader' and of 'being in control' are frequently muddled. It is impossible to be in control of a large organisation; it is vital, of course, to have distributed processes of control.

Unfortunately, there are still managers who are being trained and subsequently evaluated on ideas of scientific methods, the constant ability to solve problems and of being 'in control', and at present they are rarely questioned or challenged.

The headteacher as super-boss

There are a number of outcomes from this belief in 'efficient management', and one of them reflects back to what is expected of the leader. The leader is seen to be a 'super-manager'; it is expected that leaders must be more competent at a wider range of tasks. This model of headteacher is one of omnicompetence: the skilled classroom practitioner plus curriculum leader, plus technical expert, plus all the manifestations associated with being the figurehead and with being 'in control' of the whole mechanism all the time. It is little wonder that so many headteachers seek early retirement or suffer from a range of work-related illnesses.

The main problem is that the concept of headship outlined above and in place for some considerable time has not changed with the circumstances within which the headteacher now has to operate. At one time – a time of comparative stability or 'low turbulence' – the head was able to have all those qualities listed in the previous paragraph. The pressures and demands were very different. There was a social climate which accepted unquestioningly the one-person-in-control-and-having-the-answers version of headteacher. Now, however, the demands are very different and very much more complex and public. There is an urgent need to reconceptualise our meaning of 'headship' and the type of leader that we expect. In particular, the essentially hierarchical nature of the position needs altering.

Leadership and hierarchies

The reason why the focus is initially on the mainly hierarchical nature of headship is that such a characteristic has a direct influence on how the word 'learning' is understood in schools, and, consequently, on the role of the teacher. First, in a school culture which is not collegial, it is very difficult for teachers to see themselves as being in a partnership with their students. As happens so often in organisations, each level, not being trusted by the one above, finds it very difficult to trust the one below. Each succeeding level is in a power-coercive position to the next. A teacher is told what to do; in turn, that teacher sees him or herself responsible for getting the students to carry out their teaching instructions. As a consequence, the teacher is more likely to see him- or herself as primarily responsible for the transmission of curricular knowledge. Such a view fits, of course, with the view held centrally of the National Curriculum.

Second, hierarchies are posited on there being a high degree of certainty, on a longevity if not permanence of roles, tasks and the ultimate meaning of the institution. There is little in the way of give and take in the day-to-day ways in which the school is run. All these qualities are inimical to that openness and uncertainty which are the hallmarks of true learning. Knowing that there is a right answer to every question that arises in the running of the school tends to bolster the feeling that there is a right answer to the questions which arise in the classroom.

Third, hierarchies create a dependency culture. At every step, permission has to be asked and obtained before anything can happen. Learning is essentially about the growth of independence and self-reliance, and as such will not flourish in a hierarchical climate. The frequent complaint that students starting on their 'A' level courses do not know how to study is a symptom.

Both in terms of content and the ways in which it is transmitted in the classroom, the National Curriculum is predicated as a control culture based on there being a set of right answers. This attitude towards what officially constitutes knowledge is manifested in the often significant confusions between the functions of teaching and learning, the inference, for example, that there is a logical and causal correlation between the two, and that 'efficiency' in the former will necessarily lead to an improvement in the latter. In Chapter 3, the malign influence of the modernist's need for dichotomies was discussed, and the dichotomy of teaching/learning is one such. There is, of course, a far more complex relationship between these two words than that each simply encapsulates a separable activity. Learning can, and does, take place with or without a teacher. However, in a situation in which there is a teacher and one or more pupils, if the pupils, for whatever reason, have not learnt, then the teacher has not taught. He or she has gone through, at best, the performance of being a teacher, or has acted the role of being a teacher, but in neither case has taught. 'I cured the patient, but he died' is as logical a statement as 'I taught the pupil, but she did not learn.' The mind-set that has at its centre the idea of there being a body of inert material which can be injected into passive students can also admit of there being a causal relationship between teaching and learning which is disrupted only because the pupils are too stupid/lazy/uninterested/ awkward to learn. 'It's their fault.'

The hierarchically based mindset for leadership has a number of other implications for the implementation of learning in schools:

- automatic cohort-related chronological progression;
- time-constrained compartmentalisation;
- assessment based on 'right answers';
- emphasis on the recording of information;
- external decisions as to what constitutes knowledge.

What emerges is a picture of uniformity, dependence and an implicit definition of learning that sees it as being generic and essentially passive. Of course, this is to some extent a stereotype and a caricature, but the absence of appropriate definitions of leadership and learning allow, at the very least, the possibility of elements of what has been described to be found in some of our schools. It is certainly true that some schools are trying to chip away at the brickwork of these philosophical walls, as they recognise that the underlying culture described is not the appropriate one for the changing context in which schools are having to operate.

Schools are moving into an era which has the potential to challenge every existing premise upon which current notions of leadership and learning are posited. Four key trends can be identified:

- First, as the self-managing school movement reaches maturity, notably in England and Wales, the level of significance attached to institutional leadership and management will increase. This increase is a direct function of prevailing models of accountability which are both personal to the headteacher in terms of legal and contractual issues, and specific to the institution in terms of inspections, league tables and market share. Schools are increasingly vulnerable in that the historic support mechanisms and limited public exposure of ten or so years ago have been replaced by direct accountability to both central government and local stakeholders. The quality of decision-making at school level is becoming increasingly important as mistakes and failures are visited directly on the institution and its members. Errors or omissions in planning, budgeting and staff deployment have direct, immediate and specific consequences. Furthermore, as the leader's visibility is increased, and as his or her accountability is sharpened, so there is a powerful push to maximise the public examination results even though the majority of teachers know that there is only an accidental correlation between performance in examinations and deep learning. A good examination result, though, is frequently seen by teachers and parents as depending on 'getting through the material', an emphasis on content.

- Second, and directly related to the first point, is the increasing emphasis on 'performance', particularly at the institutional level and to a lesser degree at the personal level. There is now an overriding need for the school as a whole to demonstrate value-added, 'value-for-money', year-on-year improvement, achievement of targets, and this need has fundamentally altered the previous and long-standing view of the school as just one stage in a lifelong process, the outcomes of which may not be manifested for many years. This growing importance being attached to results, usually expressed in quantitative form, calls into question, if not actually downgrades, the view of learning as an iterative process.

- Third, these first two trends are taking place in the context of exponential social, economic and technological changes. Chapter 3 has explored these trends in detail and suggested some of the outcomes as they relate to schools. One of the major outcomes is that these changes alter the assumptions upon which schools are organised. In very simple terms, if education is a function of society and society is changing, then the a priori on which schooling is based has, at the very least, to be visited and reaffirmed, but, more probably, has to be altered in parallel. There is the strong possibility that schools will become increasingly dysfunctional because they are working to mindscapes which owe more to nineteenth-century maps of Africa (vast tracts of land labelled 'unexplored' and then turned into colonies with straight-line boundaries totally ignoring local realities) than to the latest satellite images which stress the fractal and shifting characteristics of nature.

- Fourth, and perhaps most significantly, is the growing awareness that the world is not linear but complex and chaotic. However, most prevailing orthodoxies in management and learning assume a linear and controllable universe. We looked at some of the implications of this new world in Chapter 3, but it is worth quoting from a book called *Leadership and the New Science* by M. J. Wheatley (1991):

But chaos theory has proved these assumptions false. The world is far more sensitive than we had ever thought. We may harbour the hope that we will regain predictability as soon as we learn how to account for all variables, but in fact no level of detail can ever satisfy the desire. Iteration creates powerful and unpredictable effects in non-linear systems. In complex ways that no model will ever capture, the system feeds back on itself, enfolding all that has happened, magnifying slight variances, encoding it in the system's memory – and prohibiting prediction, ever.

In our day-to-day lives in schools we recognise what Wheatley is saying – it is the dynamics of the classroom and the staff room, meetings and lessons, interviews and plans. Most importantly, Wheatley is describing the learning process in which each child in the class is a variable, and each child is made up of a complex range of variables that determine how he or she might learn. Equally, every school leader spends most of his or her time managing unpredictability, or at least reacting to it – yet this coping with the unforeseeable is rarely reflected in role descriptions or the deployment of time in the organisational structures. One of the reasons that schools can be such demanding places to work in (for both children and adults) is that people have to live in a state of permanent tension between the apparent simplicity of surface structures and the deep complexity of learning and leading.

Form follows function

If schools are not to become asynchronous, then the way that a school is led has to become a microcosm of the learning process. We need, first, to decide what the core function of the school is. It may be that many schools decide that the core function is learning; some may decide that the core function is to establish the atmosphere in which the relationships that enable learning to happen – trust, openness, lack of fear – can take root and grow. Once the core function is established, then the type of leadership needed can be established. 'Form must follow function' is a dictum in the world of technology; it needs to be one in education as well. Once the form of leadership is decided upon, then the next task is for the language that all in leadership positions use has to reflect the world in which the whole *raison d'être* of leaders is to enable all in the institution to learn. At present, much of the language in schools, the spoken language and the semiotics, puts an emphasis on teaching. Such a change in the language of the culture of the school is extremely difficult because it is a change in which the members of the community look at the world they work in. However, it is one that we all regularly engage in. Joining the staff of a school new to us, joining a club or getting married are all activities which involve developing (or realigning) our vocabularies which determine our understanding of the way we are to function, the ways we are to be together, the culture that we are to create.

Sergiovanni (1996), in his book *Leadership for the School House*, says:

The heart and soul of school culture is what people believe, the assumptions they make about how schools work, and what they consider to be true and false. These factors in turn provide a theory of acceptability that lets people know how they should behave ... Efforts to change school cultures inevitably involve changing theories of schooling and school life. (p3)

Theories are mental constructs, and as such are the product of our formulations to describe the reality that we wish to create. Much of our social understanding is created by ostensive definitions – relating a name to an object or process. The terms 'leadership' and 'learning' continue to conjure up particular processes, but these processes have in fact changed totally; the clothes of the old meanings stop us seeing the new for what they really are. This process of creating meaning is described by St Augustine in the *Confessions*, quoted by Wittgenstein (1968):

Thus, as I heard words repeatedly used in their proper places in various sentences, I gradually learnt to understand what objects they signified; and after I had trained my mouth to these signs, I used them to express my own desires. (p3)

The rest of this chapter is concerned with identifying which words should be used when we are talking and writing about leadership and learning, what are 'the proper places', and how everyone in the school can be helped to express their own desires. However, before starting this section it is vital to stress that we conceive of leadership as being dispersed throughout the organisation. It is not the prerogative of one person or of a small group. The youngest child can, if given opportunity and security, demonstrate leadership. People become trustworthy if they are trusted; people become leaders if they are given the opportunity to display leadership.

In the context of the changing world that has been described earlier in the book, and the need for leadership to be reformulated to make it logically consistent with the learning process, the following concepts are proposed:

- intellectualism;
- artistry;
- spirituality;
- moral confidence;
- subsidiarity;
- emotional intelligence.

There are two important points to be made about this list. First, there is a danger with any list – in a world that still sees things in a linear way – that a hierarchy of significance will be imposed on it. Such a hierarchy is not intended; indeed it is vital to see the six elements as interdependent and contributing to a holistic view of the nature of leadership. Second, these are all elusive concepts, each one of them subject to a variety of interpretations and applications.

A helpful metaphor is provided by Valerie Stewart (1990) in *The David Solution*:

When Michelangelo looked at the block of marble he was to carve, he looked beyond the outside and saw the shape of the statue he was to create. He could see the real beauty hidden within the waste. (p1)

Teacher as intellectual

The process of personal growth, development and change has to start with the visualisation of how we want to be; otherwise the work is that of the mason, chipping away in a mechanistic way, rather than that of the sculptor who has the guiding vision. The example of David may be an apt one for the lone artist, but a metaphor for schools to use might be from the Middle Ages and the building of a cathedral. The patron's vision had to be interpreted by and shared with the architect whose drawing had in turn to be interpreted by a wide variety of skilled workers. These workers were, of course, highly skilled and organised into Guilds, the equivalent of today's autonomous teams, and they were able to reify their part of the vision. The minutiae of specific tasks were held together and made meaningful by an overarching vision which had to be understood, shared, interpreted and translated into action.

It might seem obvious to state that the primary purpose of educational leadership is to facilitate learning, but given the complexity of the activities that are understood by the word 'learning' (*see* Chapter 4), the conflicting pressures exerted on the purposes of that learning and the dozens of ways in which the facilitation can manifest itself, then the statement points not to the obvious, but to the complexity of the task. This very complexity demands that the six concepts are interlinked – without moral confidence there can be no subsidiarity; without artistry, emotional intelligence cannot express itself; without intellectualism, spirituality can lose itself in mysticism. As in Chapter 8, the confines of a linear book are poor aids to describing non-linear interdependents.

Intellectualism

One of the most depressing outcomes of the self-managing schools movement, coupled with the introduction of a National Curriculum and its associated testing regimes, is the increasing emphasis on school leadership and management as technical skills. Increasing levels of definition, specification and imposed goal-setting have served to diminish the creative and critical components of leading and managing. Prescription of the right answers and associated models of accountability may well have contributed to the creation of an accepting and conformist culture, but such a culture is inimical to the creative learners that our society needs to cope with the next century.

Giroux (1988) argues for teachers as 'transformative intellectuals' because:

The category of intellectual is helpful in a number of ways. First, it provides a theoretical basis for examining teacher work as a form of intellectual labour, as opposed to defining it in purely instrumental or technical forms. Second, it clarifies the kinds of ideological and practical conditions necessary for teachers to function as intellectuals. Third, it helps to make clear the role teachers play in producing and legitimating various political, economic and social interests through the pedagogies they endorse and utilise.

By viewing teachers as intellectuals, we can illuminate the important idea that all human activity involves some sort of thinking. (p125)

The assertion of the teacher as intellectual is essential if the educative and transformational task of education is to be refined and strengthened. At no point in the development of educational practice – whether at national policy level or at the level of decisions about learning strategies in schools and classrooms – are there uncontentious decisions. The process of being an educator is the process of making decisions, of choosing and interpreting the outcomes in ideological and practical terms. Policies may be prescribed at a variety of levels, but the implementation of those policies involves 'forms of knowledge, language practices, social relations and values that are particular selections and exclusions from a wider culture' (Giroux, 1988, p126). Decisions as to modes of practice involve the conscious legitimisation of specific options; that legitimisation has to be an intellectual process if it is not to be reductionist, bureaucratic, and thus a denial of the deeper purposes of education as opposed to those shallow outcomes of mere training.

A further dimension to the concept of the 'teacher-as-intellectual' is that it is vital that teachers become reflective practitioners because without reflection there can be no real change, and it is very difficult to see how the notion of the reflective practitioner can be developed except in the context of an intellectual perspective. Reflective practice implies the ability to conceptualise, analyse, establish causal relationships and draw conclusions. These qualities are at the heart of effective pedagogic practice, just as they are central to the learning process, and are therefore axiomatic to any notion of leadership.

However, it must be admitted that the concept of intellectualism is not one that finds a great deal of favour in England generally, nor in the education system in particular. For a variety of reasons, the English have never been happy with the idea of intellectualism nor with the person dubbed 'intellectual'. As far as the education system is concerned, there are many people who want to reduce the status of the teacher to a craftsman at best, and to that of tradesman at worst; the idea of the teacher as intellectual is far from their thoughts. The media have for years heaped ridicule and denigration on teachers and would be unlikely to suggest that they were intellectuals. Even teachers themselves prefer not to use the word 'intellectual', preferring to use the term 'professional' instead.

It is worth quoting Said (1996) at this point, as he argues that one of the greatest barriers to the true functioning of the intellectual is the 'attitude' of professionalism:

> ... *thinking of your work as something you do for a living, between the hours of nine and five with one eye on the clock, and another cocked at what is considered to be proper professional behaviour – not rocking the boat, not straying outside the accepted paradigms or limits, making yourself marketable and above all presentable, hence uncontroversial and unpolitical and 'objective'.* (p74)

He goes on (pp76–83) to identify four characteristics which mark out the true intellectual:

- love for, and unquenchable interest in, the larger picture;
- making connections;
- refusing to specialise;
- caring for ideas and values.

Said argues that the most appropriate counter to the imperatives of specialisation, expertise, power and authority is that:

> *The intellectual today ought to be an amateur, someone who considers that to be a thinking and concerned member of society one is entitled to raise moral issues at the heart of even the most technical and professional activity* ... (p82)

For leaders in schools, Said's four points offer a powerful parallel between the qualities of leadership and the overarching educative purpose of the school. When leaders are intellectuals, they are then able to articulate the intellectual climate of the school, typify its virtues and be the model reflective practitioner. The leader has an awareness of social trends, is up to date in the relevant fields of research and cares passionately about learning. The leader as intellectual reifies the vision of the school – the school as an interpretive community creating and extending its meanings, and always challenging itself. An intellectual, self-reflective community may be uncomfortable at times, but given the moral nature and social significance of the educational process, it is essential to develop a critical and creative perspective for all in the school and one exemplified most visibly in the leader.

Artistry

One of the roles of the leader, as has been hinted at, is to interpret the best of the community back to itself and to the outside world. The leader needs to be able see beyond the roughness of everyday events to the best that is at the heart. As with nearly all metaphors, there is a limit to the length that this one can be taken. Certainly, the leader can begin the process of establishing, or re-establishing a school; the power of the vision, the passionate commitment are essential to move the plan from the map or chart into reality. Once the school settles, however, then leadership begins to emerge from every quarter, and the charismatic leader celebrates the widening concept of what it is to be a leader. The metaphor is important in that it gives the idea of there being the need in the leader at the outset to have the artist's eye to see shape where others might perceive only mass.

It is this artistic facility that is one of the differences between the leader and the manager. The manager functions within the context of the vision and makes the vision happen; the tools of management and the structures have purpose only when there is a vision to guide them. The vision, outlined first by the leader, then created by the community and finally given articulation and shape by the leader-artist, informs all that the managers do. As with so much else in education, there is no need to postulate a hierarchy between leader and manager. Is the rim or the axle more important?

The leader as artist is thus a central notion in the process of realisation – translating ideals into concrete outcomes. Leaders, in order to help formulate those ideals and to represent the community in their articulation, need three qualities that are also found in artists – vision, creativity and the ability to communicate. Those characteristics, in particular vision, are also needed in the community's search for excellence, for school improvement and for school effectiveness. Perhaps it can be said that a school *per se* cannot have a vision, only the individuals in it can. However, for a school to become a community it needs the individual visions to be garnered, moulded into a coherent shape over time and then articulated on behalf of the community. That sifting and shaping is an artistic occupation informed by the intellectual questioning, caring for ideas and values, and making connections.

The process that leads to the articulation of the vision is a complex one. In discussing the origins of the creative purpose, Gardner (1993) argues:

> At first accepting the common language of the symbol system of the domain, each creator finds soon enough that it proves inadequate in one or more respects ... because the creative individual is dissatisfied with an ad hoc solution or because the particular problem can only be solved by a fundamental reorientation ... (p33)

Given the context in which schools are increasingly having to function, and the complexity of creating a learning community, it is essential that leaders are capable of the 'fundamental reorientation' – conceptualising a new paradigm. This process is well known in the arts and the sciences – Michelangelo, Beethoven, Darwin, Einstein, Marie Curie, etc. The creativity and artistry that those people displayed are needed by our educational leaders today; certainly artistry and creativity need to be given higher significance in our understanding of what constitutes the elements of leadership. According to Henry (1991):

> Change is occurring too fast for quantitative extrapolation; rather we will have to reopen the part of us that 'knows' in some other way; the sure judge with the courage

to risk, the imagination to challenge, the sensitivity to know when to act and whom to involve. (pxi)

For Henry, creativity is:

... a thinking process associated with imagination, insight, invention, innovation, ingenuity, inspiration and illumination. (p3)

What is highly significant about this listing is that it has much in common with what happens when people learn – the creative process is one of having the intellectual and imaginative courage to make the necessary leap into understanding a new phenomenon, and this deep understanding applies equally to student, teacher and headteacher. However, if the headteacher has abdicated the creative aspect of leadership, then the community will sink back to replication, reiteration, reinforcement and resignation.

There is an obvious tension between the needs of the creative individual, at whatever position in the organisation, and the needs of the organisation itself – the need for some stability in order to support innovation. Kao (1996) uses a musical analogy, jazz improvisation, to examine the potential conflict:

A well-managed enterprise can't survive without some sheet music. It allows the management of complexity, without which the modern symphony orchestra would degenerate into cacophony. Most large-scale human interactions require their specific blue-prints, rituals, road maps, scripts, whatever, but they also require improvisation.

This chapter is not the place for a detailed discussion about creativity. However, the essential points to make are its centrality to appropriate models of leadership for learning and re-engineering and the fact that it can be developed in individuals.

The real reason why we have done so very little about creativity is very simple. We have not understood it at all. We have not understood the process of ideation. We have not understood creativity because it is impossible to do so in terms of the passive information universe ... no matter how hard we try in the wrong universe, we shall not understand creativity. (de Bono, 1991, p218)

If we are in the 'wrong universe' with regard to creativity, then the chances are that we are in the wrong universe with regard to leadership and learning. A very considerable leap of imaginative intellectualism may be needed to enable us to bring about the paradigm shift required. It will also need a high level of artistry, as we need the artist to paint a clear picture of the new world in which we are beginning to live.

The first element of artistry is the ability to communicate the new insight or vision. This ability assumes a sophisticated level of competence in order to bridge the gap between vision and understanding, and a degree of humility and patience. The first performance of Stravinsky's 'Rite of Spring' produced a riot in the audience. Stravinsky's vision was not understood and so not accepted. Many innovators experience a similar response – although riots in staff meetings are rare. Any product of a creative process will challenge existing norms and encourage new ways of thinking. In days of accelerating change, there is not the possibility of letting endless time pass passively waiting for acceptance. The leader as artist has to educate his or her audience to help them learn and understand and therefore change, has to adopt creative techniques in meetings to ensure that everyone feels free to contribute, needs to have respect for his or her intuition and that of others, and to show a passion for the expressive arts to demonstrate a belief in the multiplicity of intelligences. In these regards, the leader as artist is no different, of course, from the effective teacher.

Spirituality

One of the limitations of the competence approaches to management is that they miss the holistic view of the 'person'. Any discussion of the qualities of leadership has to address what is usually described as the 'spiritual', although this is an unsatisfactory word as it is not proposed to advocate a metaphysical or transcendental component as such. What is important is the recognition that many leaders possess what might be termed 'higher-order' perspectives. These may well be, and often are, represented by a specific religious affiliation. However, these perspectives may come from a range of sources – Covey (1992) refers to them as principles and characterises them thus:

> Principles are deep, fundamental truths, classic truths, generic common denominators. They are tightly interwoven threads running with exactness, consistency, beauty, and strength through the fabric of life.

> ... we can be secure in the knowledge that principles are bigger than people or circumstances, and that thousands of years of history have seen them triumph, time and time again. (p122)

Such principles are necessary for self-understanding; they are the means by which the individual is able to contextualise him- or herself in a chaotic, complex and often bizarrely contradictory world. A personal 'world-view' is the basis for self-awareness, of that interpretation and reflection that are the keys to personal learning and so growth through transformation.

Most educational leaders, like leaders in all walks of life, will experience failure, disappointment, frustration, rejection and hostility at some time during their professional lives. The lack of a set of fundamental principles makes such reverses impossible to bear and may give rise to acute dysfunction. When faced with personal rejection, we can either seek to reaffirm the principles by which we work, or become reactive, pragmatic and expedient. As Gardner (1995) puts it:

The creator must in some sense embody his story, although he need not be saintly . . . The individual who does not embody her messages will eventually be found out, even as the inarticulate individual who leads the exemplary life may eventually come to be appreciated. (p293)

Another writer, Terry (1993), puts the idea very clearly:

Faith in authenticity must undergird our actions . . . Leadership is spiritually grounded. (p274)

Bolman and Deal (1995) state:

Perhaps we lost our way when we forgot that the heart of leadership lies in the hearts of leaders. We fooled ourselves, thinking that sheer bravado or sophisticated analytic techniques could respond to our deepest concerns. We lost touch with a most precious gift – our spirit. (p6)

In terms of leadership development, the area of the spiritual has often been seen as being too personal or too elusive to be regarded as a significant factor. And yet, we can all remember the leader, in whatever part of the institution, who demonstrated a clear spiritual quality in his or her day-to-day life and work and who, as a result, created an atmosphere of trust and calm in which others were able to flourish. What is being suggested is not that religious faith has to be established (although a number of schools do require that information) but rather leaders need to have a clear answer to the question: 'What do you believe in?' and be equally clear in their every behaviour in answering the question: 'How do you translate your beliefs into action?'

There is no doubt that a degree of sophistication is needed to be able to articulate a belief system, and to use it as a benchmark in a variety of personal and professional contexts. Through reflection-in-action and essentially through mentoring, there can be growth and strengthening of such a system. The mentor, in particular, can help the practitioner reach a steady point, a period of 'time out'. By gentle questioning and the gift of active listening, the mentor can enable the colleague to reflect, question and probe assumptions, and test motives.

Moral confidence

This quality is clearly closely related to spirituality in that a moral code is often the most overt manifestation of any personal belief system. However, because of its significance in the context of school leadership, it requires specific elaboration.

The term 'moral confidence' is used to stress the importance attached to the capacity to act in a way that is consistent with an ethical system and is consistent over time. Such consistency requires confidence in terms of acceptance and understanding of the ethical system, and the ability to interpret it in a variety of situations. Schools are highly complex communities, but steadiness in the application of the ethical system is essential as there are no value-free decisions when adults and young people are learning together. The community is made up of people, certainly, but it is also made up of the thousands of interactions between and among people, and between people and the organisation, that happen continuously when the community is about its business. Each interaction, each time the individual and the system interact – 'moments of truth' as the Total Quality movement names it – each event must be infused by the same ethical standards that the leader articulates. If, cumulatively, a person's experience of these moments of truth gives the lie to the overt moral signals, then disillusionment and a 'switching off' will be the inevitable result. Any audit of a school could well start with an analysis of an individual's set of experiences during a day or a week to see if those experiences amount to a validation and reification of the school's expressed moral and ethical code.

The term 'consistency' was stressed at the beginning of the previous paragraph, and consistency must be tested frequently and thoroughly. It is very easy for an organisation slowly, imperceptibly to let the edges become coarser, gaps to appear, inattention to detail to become more common. At regular intervals the organisation needs to learn from itself, to be a self-reflexive organisation, essentially to see if what it says it is about is manifested in every smallest detail of its daily life.

There are two implications arising from such an audit. First it is essential that the leader creates the atmosphere in which the analysis of the community's moral consistency is seen to be of prime importance. Everyone in the school – student, support and other staff, and parents – needs to be involved, and involved because they understand the essential value of the moral core of the school. Second, the leader needs to be seen to validate her or his own actions in explicit moral terms. Indeed, self-analysis by the leader is the prerequisite to the community's ability to look critically at itself.

Sergiovanni (1996) suggests that leadership is a form of pedagogy – in basic terms 'practise what you preach' – and this way of looking at leadership captures the essence of leadership in transformed schools. At a time of moral and social uncertainty, the need for leaders to exemplify not so much a specific code, but rather the existence and understanding of a personal ethical framework, and the ability to translate that framework into validated and justified outcomes, is essential. Especially when the school as an organisation is going through turbulent times, then its moral purpose needs to be clear so that there is, for each individual in the school, a bedrock of clarity through which some sense and order can be made of the turbulence outside.

The morally confident leader can:

- demonstrate causal consistency between principle and practice;
- apply consistent principles to new situations;

- create shared understanding and a common vocabulary;
- explain and justify decisions in moral terms;
- sustain those principles over time;
- reinterpret and restate those principles in the light of the community's learning;
- discuss moral issues in leadership in all parts of the school.

Subsidiarity

It is impossible to dance if every joint is locked rigid; it is impossible to have a conversation with those who talk only in monologues; it is impossible to lead if control is seen as the overriding condition.

> *Control is an illusion. It's seductive because it gives a feeling of power. Something to hold on to. So it becomes addictive. It's hard to give up even when it's not working.* (Bolman and Deal, 1995, p31)

One of the problems with hierarchies is that they are manifested through increasing accountability which appears to require increasing capacity to control. At a time of complexity, chaos and rapid change, leadership through control will inevitably produce brittle organisations and brittle people.

The relationship between leadership, hierarchy, power and control is endemic to British organisations. If nothing else, it is reflected in the symbols of status and power – in schools manifested by unequal sharing of space and that proportion of time which is personally controlled. This well-established view has been challenged by Charles Handy (1989), who quotes a papal encyclical:

> *It is injustice, a grave evil and a disturbance of the right order for a large and higher organisation to arrogate to itself functions which can be performed efficiently by smaller and lower bodies.* (p100)

This statement is a fundamental and profound challenge to the semantics of leadership and in particular the mindscapes which inform the behaviour of headteachers and principals. Subsidiarity confronts the perceived status of headship, the assumed validity of hierarchy and the notion that delegation is a basis of effective leadership. Control and delegation, and even that new weasel-word 'empowerment', are inappropriate models for organisations that are centrally concerned with learning and that have to change rapidly. At the heart of the concept of subsidiarity is the notion of trust – willingly acknowledging that power and leadership reside in all parts of the organisation rather than 'delegating' them and then structuring organisations to institutionalise and check up on trust. Fukuyama (1995) puts it well:

> *If people who have to work together in an enterprise trust one another because they are all operating to a common set of ethical norms, doing business costs less. Such a*

society will be better able to innovate organisationally, since the high degree of trust will permit a wide variety of social relationships to emerge . . .

By contrast, people who do not trust one another will end up cooperating only under a system of formal rules and regulations, which have to be negotiated, agreed to, litigated and enforced, sometimes by coercive means. (p27)

Time and again, research and personal experience show that working in teams, self-governing teams, enables the most extraordinary results to be obtained which could not be obtained by individuals, and, equally important, sees individuals grow more rapidly than they otherwise would have. Through dialogue, in its proper meaning of genuinely thinking together, teams begin to discover what it is that stops learning, will tease out that defensiveness that blocks real progress, will eradicate all the checks to profound learning. Schools need to be about individual learning certainly, but given the world into which our children are going, they need to be about team learning as well. One of the vital roles of leadership is to ensure that teams are created and supported so that the essential of team learning can take place.

The purpose of leadership in the context of a culture of subsidiarity, or what Handy (1989) calls a federal organisation, is not to manage, but rather to enable, facilitate, interpret, create and articulate meaning, and to grow through trust.

Emotional intelligence

Emotional intelligence is, for some, a problematic concept; to many it is an oxymoron. Goleman (1996) has argued persuasively for the importance of emotional intelligence as a balance, if not an antidote, to the implicit supremacy of cognitive intelligence in the overt reward systems in school and general life.

The concept is introduced here because schools are places where the emotions play a highly significant role. Relationships between student and student, teacher and student, teacher and teacher, parent and teacher and so on are often expressed in emotional terms. Most people's memories of institutions supposedly founded on cognition and rationality are a mixture of many emotions from sheer terror to overwhelming happiness.

The process of transformation that we are arguing schools will have to go through is likely to increase the range and intensity of emotions. It therefore seems appropriate to argue for an understanding of the place of emotions in the repertoire of the leader's qualities. Being emotionally inept is as great a draw-back as being innumerate. Everyone has met the person who is said to be highly intelligent, but who manages to antagonise and hurt almost everyone who works anywhere in the vicinity. Being without interpersonal intelligence can be most disabling to the individual and the organisation.

Goleman (1996, p43) argues that emotional intelligence is made up of five domains:

1 knowing one's emotions;
2 managing emotions;
3 motivating oneself;
4 recognising emotions in others;
5 handling relationships.

Developing capability in each of these may seem an intimidating prospect, but learning in the emotional area is as possible as learning in the linguistic or mathematical.

It might be argued that developing emotional intelligence is the most complex demand that is made in this chapter. However, it is the most important. Dominating people, controlling them through rigid hierarchies and sets of rules, ensuring through fear of punishment that each person in the organisation knows his or her place and keeps to it – emotional intelligence is not needed by that sort of leader, and in fact would be a distinct handicap. The leader who sees his or her task as articulating back to the people what they know to be the best in themselves, as encouraging everyone to learn and grow, as easing from around each person any blocks to their improvement, as making the whole place celebrate success – all these attributes are essential in the world in which we live now and in the future. These attributes demand above all else a finely tuned emotional intelligence. Furthermore, emotional intelligence is vital for the development of a moral sense. Logical intelligence is needed for an understanding of legalistic rules, but the adversarial confrontation and the legalistic niceties which go alongside scrupulous administration of the law do not help young people develop a moral sense. Throughout every working day in a school there are countless incidents which can be used as exemplars of the application of a moral sense suffused with emotional, empathetic intelligence.

Leader as steward

As has been said, the list of six attributes needed by the leaders of our schools and colleges is not hierarchical. Indeed they must be seen in a holistic, interwoven pattern. Another way of looking at the requirements of our educative leaders comes towards the end of The Fifth Discipline (Senge, 1993). Here, Senge introduces the idea of the leader as 'steward'. He had interviewed a number of leaders, and saw that each understood that there was much more than merely 'running the company' in their life's work. Each saw his organisation as a vehicle for bringing learning and change into society.

Out of this deeper story and sense of purpose or destiny, the leader develops a unique relationship to his or her own personal vision. He or she becomes a steward *of the vision.* (original emphasis; p346)

The idea of stewardship takes the leader away from possessiveness – 'my school', 'my vision' – and instead forces him or her to acknowledge that the task is to be of service to a community's best view of itself. The leader is there to assist the community to learn and change and grow, but the community does not begin or end with the leader's tenure.

Steward of learning

We can apply this seminal idea to the leadership of a school. The headteacher will, first and foremost, be the steward of learning. Through personal example, in conversations, in notes to other colleagues, in some of the items in agendas for meetings, in the school magazine – in every conceivable way – the leader will demonstrate an unending commitment to learning, personal and professional. He or she will demonstrate a commitment to an intellectual, extended professionalism – self-evaluating and reflexive – that is vital if learning and growth are to occur. He or she will not merely be the principal learner, the exemplar for the school or college. He or she will ensure that the logistics are in place for learning: there will be the links with a local university, a growing professional library, a fostering of action research and a removal of clutter so that people can undertake such research, time out whenever possible, the celebration of success and encouragement when things go wrong. As the steward in the mediaeval castle ensured that the lords and ladies had all they needed for a proper life according to their lights, so the steward of the community's learning will put in place those structures that say, overtly, that here learning is vital and honoured.

Steward of the common land

Second, the principal will be the steward of the common land. A school has a number of assets which are held in common, rather like the commons surrounding the village in feudal times. In the contemporary school, the assets are the parents, the wider community of the town or neighbourhood, the business community, the schools or colleges that feed it and that it feeds. The leader will demonstrate that in today's world the school cannot be all that our children need. The subsidiarity that is explicit within the school applies equally to the community outside. It is the headteacher who has to ensure that good relations and close contacts are maintained and improved, that each can serve and help the other, and that over as short a time as possible the boundaries between school and community become so permeable that they will eventually vanish.

Steward of the boundaries

Third, the headteacher will be the steward of the boundaries, a scout picking up the signs of distant events, scanning for changes and then interpreting for the community. The headteacher will need to share with the community those ideas which are clearly going to have an impact and those which might, so that the community never sinks into the complacency of thinking that no more change need be contemplated. Scanning the boundaries is essential to ensure that the school never sits back and says, with understandable relief: 'There, we've cracked it. This is about as good a school as you can get.'

Steward of the meanings

Fourth, the principal needs to be the steward of meanings. In an interpretive community, there needs to be one person who articulates the meanings that are given to the core words and who frequently checks that the meanings are still the same. When, as they inevitably will, they alter and shift, the leader has the task of ensuring that the new meanings are truly reflective of the community, that they fit with the moral purpose and that they are generally used and accepted. As the articulator of the community's meanings, the leader must be very finely tuned to the nuances of the community's language.

Steward of good management

Fifth, the leader must ensure that there is good management – he or she has to be a steward almost in the sense that the word was used in feudal times. By 'good management' is not meant 'tight control'. The place needs to run smoothly – the leader's task in this area is to remove clutter between the individual and what needs to be done, and the removal of clutter is made easier because there is an assumption of trust. This aspect might be summed up by: 'I trust you to be your best. How can I help to ensure you are your best, and that your best is always expanding?'

Steward of celebration and story

Sixth, the leader needs to be the steward of celebration and story. A community to thrive and grow needs celebration, needs stories of heroines and heroes and of impossible challenges met, needs icons of success. The leader needs to make sure that, from the briefest smile of congratulation through to a whole-community party to welcome some overwhelmingly significant event, everyone has every triumph, every act of help and support, every show of hard work and trying, commended, acknowledged, celebrated.

Steward of the future

Finally, but as importantly and going to the heart of the word 'steward', the leader is the steward of the future. As leadership is dispersed throughout the community, the leader's task is to ensure that every possible opportunity is given for people to exercise that leadership, get help in increasing their range of abilities and attributes, and receive encouragement to go on further than they had ever dreamed possible. The present steward's responsibility is to ensure that all those potential leaders in every part of the school are ready, in turn, to become stewards in the future.

Conclusion

This chapter has set out some of the vocabulary that is needed to describe the new mind-set for leadership. If schools are to change in order to respond to a changing world, then a disjointed, incremental approach is not appropriate, if for no other reason than that it takes an inordinate toll on people. The response to profound, externally imposed change (such as the series of Education Acts over the last decade) has usually been based on piecemeal approaches derived from professional commitment – 'working harder', 'working longer'. This frenetic activity is reflected in the level of demand for retirement and the high incidence of stress-related illness. Profound and fundamental changes in what has to be done have to be met by an equally profound shift in the way it is done – and that shift has to start with the conceptualisation of leadership.

Our schools need leaders who feel at ease in a complex and chaotic world which is changing faster than at any other time in human history. They also need to embrace the idea that everyone in a school community is focused on learning, and that everyone is capable of personal transformation and growth. They need finely tuned intelligences which can cope with the complexity of people learning and changing together. Such are the qualities that leaders need in order to be able to take us into the next century.

7
■ ■ ■

In-service Development

I make two key assumptions: first, teacher education is a matter of life-long learning, starting before one enters teacher pre-service (probationary period) and continuing throughout one's career; second, teacher development and school development must go hand in hand. You cannot have one without the other. (Michael G. Fullan, Successful School Improvement)

We need the in-service development for individual teachers and for whole-school staffs to have the same rigorous theoretical underpinning, flexibility and excitement as has been suggested in Chapter 4 which looks at children's learning. We can, in fact, learn from the best practice that our young people encounter and use it to plan for the learning of adults. There will, of course, be some differences, as older people do not learn in quite the same way, nor for the same motives, and not at the same speed as children. One of the important differences is that our teachers will be learning in part for themselves, as do the children, but also and very importantly in part so that the school they work in will benefit and grow. There is, in other words, an individual and a collegial component in the learning that teachers undertake during their careers. The personal and the collegial outcomes are not necessarily in opposition. The school development plan should embrace both aspects and attempt, at least, to marry the two desires and needs as closely as possible. Moreover, the sheer involvement in the topic the teacher is learning for him- or herself will make that teacher a more interesting person. That passion will spill over into the team with which he or she is involved and, most importantly, into their contact with the students. Another benefit for the individual teacher and the school is that the many difficulties in learning, the frustrations and triumphs, the different speeds and timings, the side-alleys and diversions taken, all the vicissitudes involved will be very present to the teacher in the classroom and will be a continual reminder of the need for humility and understanding when working as coach alongside the younger learner.

Teachers as learners

The same basic features of the ways in which we help children learn will be the basis for the in-service development of teachers. Most importantly, the teachers will be learners, not people being taught; in other words, anyone involved in providing in-service education will be seen as a coach, not as the expert brought in to 'deliver' a block of knowledge that has to be learnt. Of course, there will be content, but that content needs to be seen as a starting point not as the target. In an MBA course with which the authors are involved, the first two cohorts started some two years ago. In the intervening time, there has been, in the form of papers and books to read and talks and presentations from a wide, international, variety of speakers from commerce and industry as well as from education, a very considerable volume of content. At no point, however, have there or could there have been mandated learning outcomes as a result of the content brought to the course. It has been the expectation that each member takes what he or she needs, and then adapts, moulds, interprets according to previous experience and present needs, makes individual connections between one item and another, and filters the material through a heightened self-awareness and professional reflexivity. They did not join the course to be taught but to be helped to learn. Furthermore, and very importantly, the evolving social structures of the cohorts acted as forums for learning, individuals learning from each other and allowing the socialisation to help with the filtration process vital to deep learning. At the same time, the day-to-day practice in their own schools acted as sounding boards for the new awarenesses, and in turn, the new theories were reified by the work in their schools.

There are five major aims in any programme of in-service development:

- To give teachers the chance to work to an understanding, a metacognition of what they are doing. Too often the pressures of existence, of survival, preclude the opportunity to stand back and take an overview.

- To give teachers, in school and with their peers, and on occasions with the pupils, an opportunity to explore and then demonstrate their multi-intelligences.

- To put teachers into a zone of uncertainty. The best teachers are sometimes those who, through their own uncertainties and knowledge gaps, can imagine what it is like to be a child and not know anything about the topic at all.

- To enable teachers to internalise the concept that knowledge is created.

- To enable teachers to understand how it is through relationships among equals within the domain of a topic area's discipline that knowledge is created and deeply learnt.

Looking for coaches

To begin with the second and last points above: the school will need to choose those who help with in-service development very carefully, whether those people come from inside or outside the school. Essentially the school will be looking for coaches. These coaches will be very aware of the non-linear ways in which people learn, and of the different intelligences that they bring to bear on the topic. The coaches will create time and space for the physical movement that some need in their learning – the vigorous walk or the dance or the swim which the mind needs the body to perform while the new ideas are being explored and sorted; they will make time for the physical representation, through mime or drama or dance, of some new learning; they will help the visually intelligent to make the shapes and forms that reify the topic; they will, above all else, allow time for the inter- and intrapersonal creation of meaning.

They will also ensure that there is blend of individual and team learning. As schools increasingly recognise the importance of team working, there will need to be a parallel development of team learning. There will need to be a balance between the common learning needed for the growth of the school and the encouragement of individual differences within that framework. As with so much in this book, we are not suggesting a dichotomy; an individual's learning will feed into the team's activities, and what the individual learns from working in a team will broaden his or her professional and personal horizons. In addition, there is that added dimension and dynamic to learning in a group, knowing that the learning will be put to use in furtherance of the team's aims.

In short, there will be approaches which are as subtle and varied as the people who are attending. There will also be a variety of timings, as the speed of acceptance of the evolving new understanding will not be the same for all. The slow, gentle spiral around the topic might suit one person; the quick dash to meaning might be best for another.

Essential curiosity

How is the curiosity of those involved aroused and, equally importantly, sustained, as without curiosity there will be no motivation? Again, the relationships between those taking part is at the core. It takes time and empathetic, active listening to find out what sparks an individual's curiosity. Curiosity is essential, but it is joyously unpredictable, and the in-service development programme that allows for no wild wanderings is not worth the attending. And, once that curiosity is aroused, how is the sheer serendipity which comes from exploring new ideas, which is a central part of learning, acknowledged and encouraged? No learner goes from A to B to C through to the end of the neatly linear textbook. A chance sighting, a curious colour at the edge of vision, an unexpected tingle of excitement at some new insight, and the true learner is off on a track unthought of by textbook, teacher or learner. Staff development that tries to imprison the learner into a pre-packed topic is doomed. Again, and it is necessary to stress this point, it is the scaffold of a trusting relationship that allows for a grand variety of buildings to take shape.

Adult mind-maps

Children will learn at a deep level only if the concept being introduced is carefully fitted to the existing mind-map. So with adults. However brilliant the lecturer, however well-researched and documented the topic, if what is being said goes against the experienced reality of the learner, no learning will take place. The 'lecturer' has to go through a metamorphosis – he or she has to become a coach, a mentor, but still acknowledged as one who brings a new perspective, and fresh slant.

The role of the coach

There has to be time first to explore in an atmosphere of trust the map that the learner brings. There has to be time for that necessary mixture of gentle probing and rigorous intellectual challenge which encourages and urges the learner to explore his or her own deeply held feelings on the topic, and openly share those ideas, that reality; of course, this exploration is one from which the coach will learn. Then, the outlines of the new idea or the different approach have to be explored, again in trust, by both coach and learner. Then, and over a period of time, the learner has to see if he or she is comfortable with the new idea, and if so, there will be a shift in perceptions, in his or her reality, to accept the new concept. If there is a feeling of discomfort, the new idea will be rejected as surely as the body rejects a mismatched donated organ. It needs to be remembered at all times that the lecturer/coach is not bringing a higher reality; there is no 'better' truth being held in front of the learner which she would be stupid or pig-headed to reject. The coach may feel that this approach is better than that, that this new research shows conclusively that the old ways are wrong, that this insight must be taken on by all who are shown it, but he or she will have to curb such impatience and wait to see if this alternative reality is accepted.

While this process is under way, the teacher is experiencing two other, parallel, activities. These activities might be, at first, unconscious, but within a short time the coach needs to bring them to the forefront and discuss them. The first is that the teacher enters the 'zone of uncertainty'. The teacher is being helped by the coach to look at a topic from a different vantage point from the one he or she is accustomed to. A number of emotions may be stirred: unease, irritation or even anger, disbelief, rejection; old, well-known certainties are being eroded; aspects of the teacher's own self are being scrutinised. This uncertainty is, of course, what children feel so often, but it is not merely to remind teachers of what children experience that they need to go through this zone, but, as we explain later in this chapter, it is because schools are, in a world of very considerable uncertainty, overly certain places. This zone is also a reminder that learning is frequently uncomfortable, even agonising, and that while we are going through it, we require a holding-frame which does two things simultaneously. It provides gentle acceptance, a sense of trust; but it also challenges, pushes each individual to the most rigorous thinking and questioning. The two types of support are vital to each other, either on its own being inadequate.

The reflexive practitioner

However, the teacher cannot be left uncertain, cannot be left in limbo. The coach and teacher together internalise, argue through, adapt and shape the new idea or approach and, at the end of the process, land once more into certainty. At the same time as this journey is undertaken, the coach needs to help the teacher see what is happening; together they need to stand back from the process, take the emotions out and examine them, test the old ideas, probe the assumptions underlying them. Together, teacher and coach lift above the process and understand it from outside; metacognition becomes possible and, as the process is repeated many times, becomes a standard part of the teacher's and coach's way of looking at their professional lives. Together they become reflexive, extended professionals. One outcome of this metacognition will be the sudden realisation that together they have created 'knowledge' – neither has accepted simply and without debate an imperative from a textbook or a lecturer's talk. The idea has been talked through, the past experience and emotions of both have helped shape the idea; what they reach at the end of the process has been *made*, not given.

It is, perhaps, dangerously near stating the glaringly obvious that the process described above is one that needs to be carried over into the classroom. Certainly, if it is a process that the teacher has not experienced it will be enormously difficult, if not impossible, to create the atmosphere in the classroom in which such a dialogic creation of knowledge can take place. It is for that very reason that the stress throughout this chapter is on in-service development and education, and not on training.

Training versus development

It is worth breaking off at this point to look at the word 'inset' (ie 'in-service training') and in particular at the 'training' element in it. The fact that 'training' is mentioned is indicative of much that has been wrong. Too often, what has occurred under the label of 'inset' has been a one-off introduction to a particular technique or approach. There are, of course, certain occasions when such a skills-based inset day is appropriate; there is a need for this teacher to upgrade their skills in word-processing; that teacher wants to be instructed in how to use a new machine in the design area; another needs to see the new range of audio-visual material for the teaching of French. Further, there are occasions when a lecturer can be stimulating and introduce the staff to a new trend or idea, but then there must be time for going over the territory at a later date and for each member of staff to explore the ideas; if such mulling over does not take place there is little chance of there being any lasting impact. However, both these types of inset should make up only a very small proportion of the time that the staff spends in continuing education, and indeed instead of 'inset' we might look to establishing a new acronym: 'insconted' (with its faint echo of divine discontent in the background) – in-service continuing education. The emphasis needs to be on the continuing renewal of the teachers by involvement in their own, expanding education.

We want to put forward two very broad categories of continuing education. The first is based on the school's own investigations into its workings – the school audit. In brief, the school looks at its aims and vision, then investigates very closely an aspect of the day-to-day implementation of that vision, discovers if there are gaps and then organises in-service education which directly deals with the gaps. The second arises from a need that all organisations have – to return, at fairly regular intervals, to their roots and to ask, and answer, the fundamental question: 'Why are we doing what we are doing?' Once again we are up against the limitations of a linear book; these two approaches take place in tandem, overlapping and informing each other. There, again, is no hierarchy in their importance; both are vital to the well-being of the institution. Both are aimed at eliminating that major block to any institution's growth and transformation – lack of reflection. By 'lack of reflection' is meant that the need for sheer survival and the anxiety naturally felt by everyone in the organisation that the machinery must be kept going at all costs together make it very easy indeed to forget why the enterprise was started in the first place. The first activity that is suggested is aimed at the question: 'Is what we are doing the best that we can do?' The second is aimed at the question: 'What are the core beliefs that inform and give soul to this organisation?'

As learners, the teachers need to be involved in choosing the topic of the inset, its timing, its location. The topic must arise from the analysed strengths and needs of the staff, and not be imposed by a hierarchy, be that inside or outside the school. Unless the teachers are thoroughly involved, there will be little deep involvement in what happens. Again, the parallel with children's learning is close. Putting a textbook in front of each member of the class and saying that the contents of that textbook is what is going to be learnt is no guarantee of an enthusiastic response. Similarly, if a notice goes on the staff room board saying that there will be a session on such and such a topic, there is no guarantee of a rapt interest.

A starting point

Let us examine a specific example: A school has recently been inspected, and in the published report there is criticism of the pastoral system. The headteacher, with or without the senior management team, then decides that clearly there is need for inset on 'How to make your pastoral system successful'. He asks the deputy in charge of inset to make the arrangements, and the staff is duly notified of the time and place. A pastoral 'expert' is found, and duly lectures the whole staff on how to run a pastoral system. There could hardly be a more disastrous start.

First, such a move says to the staff that the 'boss knows best'; the decision and the way it is conveyed are both patronising and autocratic. The top-down approach will obtain conformity but not commitment. Second, it accepts without question the inspectors' division of the school into a 'curriculum' section and a 'pastoral' section, a dichotomy which many schools are trying to put behind them. Third, it gives to the inspection report the authority of holy writ. It may well be that there is very little wrong with the system, and the school could put right the little that is wrong without any resort to whole-school inset. Fourth, it misses the opportunity for involving the staff in carrying out an audit to find out if there is a problem, and if there is, what form it takes and then deciding on the basis of that knowledge what sorts of in-service education would be most appropriate. In other words, the report need not be taken as infallible, but it can act as a trigger for the school to make a thorough investigation of itself.

The audit

Carrying out an internal, school-controlled audit is the most powerful tool in pointing to what in-service education is needed, and the audit itself is highly effective education in itself.

Given the starting point of the inspection report's finding, the school could follow this course of action. The headteacher and the senior management team, at a staff meeting following the inspection, discuss with the staff the comments that the inspectors made at the time of reporting back to the SMT, and if there were any other people, such as year heads, involved in that report-back they would join in the discussion of what they thought the inspectors said. Other members of staff would relate what conversations took place with inspectors looking at pastoral matters, and would also comment on the sorts of reactions inspectors appeared to be making. When the inspectors' comments behind the written comment had been looked at, the staff would then admit that there was, on the face of it, a case to be answered in that there had not always been satisfaction with the way in which pupils' problems had been dealt with. The staff further decides that, for the purpose of this exercise, the artificial separation of 'curricular' and 'pastoral' would be accepted. In this way, the staff is involved in establishing its right to probe an area to which its attention has been drawn, and take the appropriate course of action arising from its own investigation. The most applicable approach would be the focused audit, and as the school has carried out audits in the past, it is decided by the staff to set one up.

The next step might be for a small working party to volunteer to establish the methodology to be followed and to report back to the whole staff in three weeks. Ideally the working party would consist of a broad spectrum of the staff. Its first step would be to write the hypothesis to be tested. It would be of little use to have one as wide as: 'There is a problem with the pastoral system'. The working party, taking into account the discussion at the staff meeting, decides that the hypothesis would be: 'The pastoral system reacts well to perceived crises, but does little to try to prevent them.' At a brief staff meeting, the working party checks that this hypothesis is agreeable to the staff.

Following the establishment of the hypothesis to be investigated, it would be necessary to look at the stated aims and objectives of the school and the mission statement, to pick out the underlying principles that the school says guide the ways it attempts to look after the students. These criteria would provide the first series of questions: How well are these criteria known? Are they universally understood? Are they universally agreed with?

Next, the data that were needed to be collected would be specified. What sort of data would prove or disprove the hypothesis? Among the positive data could be the numbers of cases in which children had manifestly been in some sort of trouble and had been helped in part or totally by someone acting in a pastoral capacity. Among the negative data could be examples of bullying that had not been discovered until a victim had been badly hurt; the numbers of students unhappy with a teacher but no one intervening in time, with the result that students' work deteriorated; parental complaints that children had been 'picked on' by members of staff and/or other pupils, but with no subsequent evidence of anyone intervening.

The next stage would be stating from where, and how, the data would be gathered. In this case, the data would come from the records kept on the children, from questionnaires to children and parents, and from semi-structured interviews with a selection of teachers and children.

Finally, it would be necessary to decide how best to report back the findings, and to fix a time-limit within which to work.

The outcomes of the audit

At first sight, such a process might seem to be a competent way of dealing with a finding by the inspectors, but having little to do with in-service education. However, the carrying out of the working party's remit would in fact be a powerful and focused piece of learning for the whole staff. First, it would start the investigation of the meaning of the language of the institution, and in the next chapter we show how this is the first step to institutional growth. Next, by looking at the criteria, it would force staff to think about how far they know and implement those criteria. Where there was a gap between intention and implementation, there could be a focus point for further study. The gap would be challenged by questions: Is the gap due to ignorance of the criteria, and if so how can that best be eliminated? Is the gap caused by poor communication, and if so what does the institution need to do to improve it? Is the gap caused by the staff's lack of knowledge about how to carry out the intentions?

By collecting data, the school begins properly to examine itself, to reflect on what it is doing and how it is doing it. A general reflection on practice is the start to the individual reflective practitioner, and it is to that state that all in-service education should be heading. As with the examination of the criteria, careful scrutiny of the data will show if there are failures in the stated procedures. If the questionnaire shows, for example, that a number of students say that they have been consistently bullied, there will again be a clear focus point for the staff to consider how they need to reinforce relationships so that children felt free to talk with teachers about such topics. Finally, the written report that emerged at the end of the process would, or could, be a blueprint for further development.

The above example is used to stress the need for inset to emerge from a clear picture, known by all the staff, of where the school is at any point, and what is needed to move the school closer to its ideals. In this way, each teacher will feel involved, and will want to take part and contribute. Moreover, the audit will reveal individual teachers' strengths, and these people will be able to act as tutors in future inset work. The identification of these tutors will help fulfil another requirement of inset, which is that it should be as much in-house as possible. If there is insufficient strength in the school, then an outsider will be invited to help, but the outsider will be filling a gap identified by the school, and contributing in ways identified by the school.

Action research

Another way in which the proposed inset can be rooted in the real needs of the school is as an outcome of Action Research (AR). In a growing number of schools, teachers are undertaking AR as a part of a degree jointly organised by the school and the local university. The topics that are chosen in such AR are immensely varied and each can act as a focus for inset. For example, in a recent piece of AR, a teacher looked at the possible relationship between the class-room layout and the degree of involvement by the pupils in the mathematics lessons. The results were most interesting, and the remainder of the depart-ment was then drawn in to further investigation. Clearly, such a topic could well be taken up by the remainder of the school, with the initial teacher being the lead figure in the application of his or her methodology to other situations.

The above example of AR highlights a vital aspect of this form of in-service education: it originates in the school and is driven by a particular teacher's interest or curiosity, but it is validated and possibly helped by the link with an outside body, such as a university. In this way, there is a symbiotic link between theory and practice, between the practical day-to-day concerns of a teacher or department on the one hand, and the researchers' theories and methodologies on the other. The theory illuminates and shapes the practice, and the practice gives flesh and life to the theory. Too often, educational research is seen by practising teachers as being remote from their concerns; through AR, the gap is bridged, and the learning that results is well rooted and therefore effective. Furthermore, the study is directed at a very particular aspect of the school's work, rather than attempting to tackle a broad and poorly focused area.

Teams

In those areas of a school's work where it has been identified that teams rather than individuals be responsible, then it is vital that the team undertake in-service education together. There is very little to be gained, and a very great deal to be lost, in taking the team leader out of school for the day to be lectured about how to lead a team. The team leader needs to learn with the team, and all of them begin the process of learning how to work as a team. Equally, when the team does train together, then the outcomes need to be discernible; at the end of the sessions, the team needs to be able to do something that it could not have done previously.

The competency movement

The greatest danger in current trends in inset is the drive to reduce complex and interrelated matters to simplistic bits. As with the curriculum which has been atomised into quite spurious subject compartments, so management and leadership, key features in a transforming school, have been reduced to 'competencies'. The drive behind such reductionism is to ensure that the process of producing the next generation of managers is made simpler, controllable and testable. The flaw with the modernist, bureaucratic theory is that it ignores the fact that the whole is much more than the sum of the parts, and being so, is far more difficult to replicate and impossible to reduce to a checklist. In very simple terms, what the competency movement has attempted to do is identify a number of, for example, headteachers who are reckoned to be superior headteachers, and by shadowing them for some time produce a list of the competencies that they are supposed to have demonstrated. The list can then be taken over by a trainer, and a group of aspiring heads can be drilled through the list, emerging, so the theory goes, at the end of the course with the necessary baggage needed to become a successful head. The competencies are labelled 'generic', and it is supposed that by so labelling them the competencies do in fact become transportable from one situation to another.

The fallacy of this approach may best be shown by looking at an example from the performing arts. A few years ago, when he was at the height of his powers, it was decided to identify the competencies displayed by Rudolph Nureyev so that a future generation of Nureyevs could be ensured. Every aspect of his dancing, training and diet was analysed. Films were made so that each movement could be broken down into the minutest detail. No aspect of his technique was left unnoted. The items were listed, put in some sort of sequence and handed over to the teachers of ballet, and they started to drill the new generation. 'Do these movements exactly as he did and you will become another Nureyev.'

As soon as one reads such an idea, its utter preposterousness becomes self-evident. Nureyev certainly possessed some 'generic' skills; in ballet there are skills without which you simply cannot become a dancer. However, he also possessed some 'genetic' skills, and they made him the extraordinary and irreplaceable dancer that he was. His ability was to transcend the generic skills. He transmuted basic skills into a sublime art form. Furthermore, he relied on others to add their artistry, and the performance depended on the chemistry of numbers of people giving to and receiving from each other. With a different group of people on a different stage, with a different audience, there was a different performance. He was not a robot; you could not replicate him or program him to function identically at every performance because of his 'generic' skills. So it is with outstanding headteachers.

Peter B. Vaill (1989), in *The Manager's Bookshelf*, ed. Pierce and Newstrom (1996), summed up very neatly the differences between the assumptions underlying the competency movement (CM), and the counter-arguments:

CM assumptions	Counter-arguments
Competencies are distinct and independent	Competencies exist in clusters
Managers produce identifiable outputs from the exercise of various competencies	Not all managers produce identifiable, physical outputs related to competencies
Increased organisational effectiveness is greatly influenced by competencies	Organisational effectiveness is effected by many more important factors than managerial competencies
Managers create and/or restore order	Managers must be innovators and creators of disorder
Possessing a competency implies knowing when, where and how to use it	Perceptions distort judgments about when, where and how to use a competency

Competencies can be used regardless of the party who is the target of this use	Interaction with others influences the effectiveness of competency usage
No untoward effects of correct competency use on the system will occur. If they do, competencies to deal with these can be learned	Even the correct use of a competency can create systemic problems

In-service 'training' – and the word is used deliberately – in the educational world that pretends to pass on abstracted skills whether of leadership, management or pedagogy is flawed and malign. It is part of the movement which is concerned first with reducing the profession to a craft at best and a trade at worst, and second with maintaining a strict and central control. By following this reductionist line, it is possible to show that there is nothing special about being a teacher or headteacher. After all, so the argument goes, the skills of a leader in education can be itemised and 'delivered' in a training session. Similarly, once such a list is established, it is possible to produce a checklist against which a headteacher can be graded as conforming or not.

Conclusion

Of course, in-service development and education for teachers and headteachers is essential. However, such development is facilitated, mentored, encouraged; it is not taught. Anyone involved as the facilitating outsider can most certainly ask probing questions, can bring a fresh eye and new thinking to a situation, can be the critical friend. To be of any lasting worth, however, the school-based studies must be seen as part of a never-ending extension of the professionalism of the people concerned, and as enlarging their abilities to improve the school. Therefore, in-service development must be embedded in the value system of the institution in which the individual teacher works as part of a team; it must reflect the particular vision of that school or college, and be part of achieving it. It must flow from, and lead back to, the relationships that created the need for the development in the first place. In other words, in-service development is not a 'bolt-on' undertaken in a vacuum. It would be a considerable help to a proper understanding of what the process should be if the term 'inset' were dropped and in its place was put the phrase 'professional development' or, perhaps, our new word: 'insconted'.

The second approach to in-service development is for the institution to go back to its roots, to rediscover what it is that it truly believes in, what constitutes its soul. What follows are some questions or topics that might be considered starting points. The list does not even attempt to be exhaustive; it is merely some suggestions which any school deciding to undertake this activity needs to adapt to its own particular circumstances.

- 'Schools need to raise their standards.' Exhortations of this type have been directed at schools for some time. Leaving aside the confusion in the word 'standards', the moral purpose is also totally unclear. One has to ask: 'To what end?' Are we in education to raise our students' standards the better to take their place in a consumer society, and the better to produce goods for that society? Or are we to raise those standards among our students that help them pose the questions, and attempt answers, as to why the top 5 per cent of the population of the UK holds 51 per cent of the wealth? why in one part of the UK the average weekly wage is £255 and in another £450? why one third of children live at or below the official poverty line? why a disproportionate number of black children end up in 'remedial' classes or 'sin-bins'? what quality of human spirit enables people to bring down the Berlin Wall, or brave Soviet tanks in Budapest? why 20 per cent of the world's population is using 80 per cent of the finite resources? The argument is not against greater literacy and numeracy. The argument is that mere mechanical prowess is an insufficient achievement to inspire our young people.

  > ... by the year 2000 we should be number one in the world in the percentage of eighteen year olds that are politically and socially involved. Far more important than our mathematics and our science scores is the involvement of the next generation in maintaining our democracy and helping those within it who need assistance ... Schools that cannot turn out politically active and socially helpful citizens should be identified and their rates of failure announced in the newspapers. (Berliner quoted by MacDonald, 1996)

  The question, therefore, needs to be put: 'Are we enabling our students to ask those questions, and to begin to find routes to their answers, that will enable them to play a moral role in a vibrant democracy?'

- 'More is less.' Mies van der Rohe used this comment about architecture, but it applies with equal force to learning. If pupils are not given the time to explore, fit new ideas into old schemata, filter and adjust, they will learn only at the most superficial level. The next question, therefore, is a threefold one: 'Are we about deep learning or shallow learning? If the former, how are we to organise classroom time so that with our pupils we can, together, explore in depth? How can we convince ourselves and all our clients that such deep coverage will better serve both the short-term examination needs of our pupils and their long-term ability to be life-long learners?'

- In a world of uncertainty, and one in which there are many more wrong answers than there are right, schools are immensely certain and insistent on right answers. We need to look for ways in which schools can provide on the one hand the emotional stability that all children need when growing up, and on the other the ability and enthusiasm to cope with immense change, continuing uncertainty and few 'right' answers. The next question might be: 'How do we enable our classrooms to be nursery gardens in which questioning flourishes and intellectual uncertainty is seen to be enormously stimulating?'

- John Seeley Brown *et al*, quoted by Bruner (1996), speak of intelligence as not being simply 'in the head' but as 'distributed in the person's world' – 'the reference books one uses, the notes one habitually takes, the computer programs and data bases one relies upon, and perhaps, most important of all, the network of friends, colleagues or mentors on whom one leans for feedback, help, advice, even just for company.' The next question might be: 'How do we make sure that our school ensures the widest possible distribution of human and non-human resources so that each child's intelligences are able to grow to their maximum?'

- Finally – 'form follows function'. Schools need to look at the fundamental structures of their staffing, timetabling, grouping of subjects, room allocations, times of the school day – every aspect of their organisations – to see if they are in place directly to help children learn or for purposes of control and administrative ease. The final question in this list, therefore, is: 'Does every single facet of our structures reflect that overriding commitment we have to enable each child to learn to her or his maximum?'

8
■ ■ ■

Transforming Schools

Through learning we re-create ourselves. Through learning we become able to do something we were never able to do. Through learning we reperceive the world and our relationship to it. Through learning we extend our capacity to create, to be part of the generative process of life. (Peter Senge, *The Fifth Discipline*)

Were it to be humanly possible to do so, it would be recommended that this chapter be read simultaneously with the previous one on in-service development. The two topics, that of changing the culture of a school so that it can respond to new sets of demands and the in-service development that needs to be put in place so that teachers become extended, reflexive professionals accepting and welcoming of change, work in tandem. The former, changing the culture, depends in large part on the latter, and the guiding principles and direction of the in-service development are set by the former. Unfortunately, we are up against the restrictions of the linear book; nevertheless, as the reader takes on these two chapters, we hope that their twin-like nature will be remembered.

To transform schools is to transform cultures. In transforming cultures, people change the meaning that they give to themselves and to the institution in which they work. To transform a school, therefore, is not merely to change the structures. One of the major messages of this book is that 'form follows function', and it follows from this dictum that any change that an institution decides to undertake depends in the first instance on a clear definition of its function. Certainly, there are some structures that inhibit change or that make it entirely impossible. A rigid autocracy, for example, looks on change as a threat to its continued existence and will fight it ruthlessly. It is equally certain, as a great deal of research from the United States has shown, that merely changing structures makes no difference to the essential culture of a school. Once the need for change has been recognised, then it is the culture of the school that is the first and chief area for investigation, not the possible structures that might be put in place at a later date. The structures will emerge from the types of activities that the transformed school sees as its core functions.

The group's mind-set

Another way of elucidating the 'culture' of a school is to view it as the mind-set of the people who work there. The mind-set is the sum of the usually unarticulated reactions to the key words which describe the thing that we call a school. Three, of very many, such words are: 'teach', 'learn' and, of course, 'school'. Schools have for a very long time seen themselves, and been seen by the society they serve, essentially as institutions in which a group of adults *teach* younger people; the younger people, in turn, see themselves as *learners*. These two words have been frequently understood to be in a dichotomous relationship, or to be separate activities each capable of functioning independently of the other. We have said elsewhere that learning is certainly possible without any teacher being there. We have only to think of the massive learning a child undertakes, successfully, in the first few years of his or her life to be aware of the truth of that statement. However, it is impossible for teaching to have taken place if there has been no learning. It is possible to hear people say that the lesson had been a very good one, that he or she had taught very well, but unfortunately some or all of the pupils had not learnt anything. A focus on teacher as performer and on child as passive recipient allowed the activity of teaching to exist almost in a vacuum, quite separate from the reaction of the people for whom the exercise was put in place. In short, the dominant mind-set is that a school is somewhere in which adults do something to children; teachers are active but children are merely reactive to teacher stimuli. At the end of a time there, children know how to be taught, but may not necessarily know how to learn. The transformational school is about changing this situation completely; a school must become a place in which everyone learns how to learn, and in which each person is helped to be the initiator in his or her own learning.

Teacher and learner

Furthermore, there is a hierarchical implication behind the pair of words; clearly a teacher is in a superior position to the learner. Part of the emotional surround to the word 'learner' is the feeling that there is something juvenile about being in that position; the learner is dependent on the teacher and will eventually grow up and display a capability that he or she did not have previously. The rich store of jokes and cartoons about 'learner drivers', about still having 'your L-plates' on, is testimony to the idea that learners are potentially dangerous and certainly have less standing in the community than teachers. The pejorative undertone to the word, the idea that a learner is incomplete, still in the process of becoming, distances even further the learner from the teacher. The latter is established, has a clear role, is complete. This completeness brings with it a sense of certainty. Teaching implies knowing something, and knowing something, in the language of schools, all too frequently means being certain about it. The problem is that in a world of increasing uncertainty, expressions of certainty are out of joint. Certainty implies that there is body of knowledge 'out there' that the teacher has reached, but that the learner is still trying for. In fact, however, teacher and learner together need to make a temporary sense of matters that are in continuous flux, and learner and teacher together need to be developing that sense of cheerful acceptance that there is no certainty. Teacher and learner together create a dynamic knowledge, a knowledge that flows and eddies between the two, each adding and learning from the other. At any given moment it might be difficult to discern who is teacher and who learner.

Teacher as learner

The perceived clarity of the teaching role is an additional barrier between the teacher and the learner. Clearly, the teacher has been trained, and has been accredited as a 'teacher'; such a label is, barring any major changes or disasters, attached to the person until retirement. The learner is 'just a learner' until the learning ends and then he or she becomes something else, but while the process goes on, that person is seen as a recipient of the teaching. Once it is accepted that a teacher is also a learner, then it will be vital to explore the reciprocity of learning between teacher and student.

Teacher as isolate

To transform a school so that it becomes a learning institution, therefore, is to attempt to change deeply held meanings of and emotional reactions to words that go to the fundamentals of what gives a person a sense of identity. Teachers, more than any other profession possibly, spend a great deal of their time working in isolation. The bureaucratic architecture of a school, with 'the curriculum' broken down into small parcels and individuals being given the responsibility for dealing with one parcel, then carrying out that duty in a closed room, all contribute to isolation. The very geography of school buildings reifies the idea that the teacher and his or her class work together unvisited and unobserved. The team-teaching popular in some schools in the 1970s and the imposition of the appraisal system have had some impact on this isolation.

However, the National Curriculum's insistence on separate subject labels has not promoted team-teaching; in addition, the very small total number of hours when a teacher is observed as part of the appraisal system means that, in effect, most teachers for most of the time operate in a closed classroom.

Such isolation has a number of effects, the chief of which is that the personality of the teacher and the activity that he or she carries out become increasingly indivisible. The person is the teacher; the teacher is the person. To change the teacher is to change the person. The outsider may see the proposed change as a mere readjustment of a routine, the addition or deletion of a particular activity. The teacher can see it as a suggestion that his or her personality is in some way deficient, and an activity that has been carried out for years, that is seen as an integral part of the total package that makes up 'me-as-teacher/person', is being adversely criticised.

However, the need to change what schools do and how they do it is urgent, and schools are made up, *inter alia*, of teachers, so that in saying that schools need to change, the clear implication is that teachers need to change. To achieve that, there must be an overwhelming and clear reason, understood by all, why change needs to take place.

Why change?

That clear reason can come from a number of external and internal sources. One of those sources is the certainty, expounded in Chapter 3, that schools simply cannot continue operating on the basis of nineteenth-century assumptions and still have credibility in the eyes of children who will live in the twenty-first century. A more immediate prod, and perhaps the best known one at present, is Ofsted and its system of inspections. Another arises from the league tables of examination and test results that might persuade parents not to send their children to a particular school; the prospect of falling numbers is a sharp incentive for the school to change. Internal sources which prompt change can come from a general feeling that 'we can do better', from the arrival of a new headteacher who sees areas for renewal and change, or from a critical friend of the school, who straddles the internal–external divide and can help the school sharpen its knowledge of itself.

In the background to all these sources there is a generally agreed notion of what a 'good school' looks like, what its determining features are. The conventional wisdom looks to researchers such as *Ten Good Schools* (DES, 1977), Rutter, Reynolds, Mortimore and many others, and their ideas coalesce into that list of features of the effective school by now very well known: the 'strong' leader, consistently high expectations, clear goals and so on. However, knowing that change is necessary, and knowing that there is a body of research which points to a number of models that might be used, may not be sufficient to overcome that inertia which is an inevitable part of any organisation. Some catalyst, some initial spur is needed.

Leader as change agent

The first step, the essential trigger without which little if anything will move, is for the leader bravely and with compelling clarity to explain why radical change is necessary. This is one of the responsibilities inherent in being the leader – he or she has to be the chief analyst. It is the role of the leader continuously to scan the boundaries, the lands outside the school, to monitor what is happening, to pick out those trends and shifts which will have an impact on the students and teachers in the school. He or she then has to translate those major trends into the language and culture of the school, and elucidate the vision of how the school can change and develop in order to cope with the impending external changes. There are many disincentives facing the leader. One is that over recent years there have been so many changes imposed from the centre that there is a natural inclination to cry 'No more!' Schools, however, cannot be shielded from the general imperative to match their methods of operating to the vastly increasing possibilities that are present in the world.

Another more insidious disincentive, and one that comes from within the school, is that if the school feels itself to be successful, sees itself attracting children and parents, has a good standing in the community – is, in other words, strong enough to change – then the temptation is to say that there is manifestly no need for change. At the other end of the scale, the school that sees itself as being unpopular finds it very difficult indeed to summon up the morale and energy and gather the necessary human and material resources in order to undertake the radical change that it knows to be necessary. Handy (1994) shows in his illustration of the sigmoid curve how the best motivation and springboard for change is when an institution is at the peak of its strength. The school in a strong position has only two ways to go – either to take courage and change and improve, or not to change and start the inevitable decline. The option of staying still does not exist. If the school is weak, then there is no doubt that radical change is far more difficult, but a leader in such a position will focus on the small steps of immediate improvement, but with the distant vision as guide and inspiration.

The need for trust

The second stage in the transformational process is the establishment of an atmosphere of trust in which everyone can openly examine the meanings that they have given implicitly and over a long period of time to the words that carry the deep foundations of their culture. Such an examination cannot be ordered from outside; it cannot even be commanded by the peak of a hierarchy within the school. It must arise from a genuine desire of the staff of the school to change, to transform itself. The leader has begun the process, developed it and taken part in the formal and informal discussions, and at the end of this two-way exchange, he or she both articulates what the staff has decided to do and sketches out a chart of how it is to be done. Such a wish to change implies a very great deal of trust among the members of the school. There is no way in which a school can undertake the necessary audits, investigations and open questioning of everything it does unless everyone can be totally open with one another.

However, it is easy to suggest that schools need to establish an atmosphere of trust, but it is far more difficult for schools to start that process. The difficulties are many, but perhaps the overriding one is that teachers have been the target of a sustained and at times vitriolic campaign of denigration, one that has dented the sense of professionalism and the self-esteem that are crucial to an open and probing debate. The leader's task, therefore, is to reinforce at every possible opportunity the teachers' self-esteem. In the same way that people become trustworthy only when they are trusted, so people will act as professionals only when they are treated as professionals. That sentence, however, is open to misinterpretation. Some have used the term 'professional' as an escape route, a cover for saying that it is acceptable to continue acting in isolation; to 'be a professional' can mean to some a desire to be left alone, to act not as a member of a team but singularly. In the context of the transformational school, however, to act professionally means to put the children's and adults' learning at the centre of the corporate activity, and to extend each individual's ability and self-knowledge the better to carry out the task of the institution.

The other major barrier to an open dialogue in trust is the understandable hesitancy in probing colleagues' deeply held beliefs. It is easier, more 'collegial' in the wrong use of that term, to let sleeping opinions and attitudes be. It is less stressful on the nerves. That barrier has to be broken. At first on a one-to-one basis, and then in the teams that are to be the cornerstone of the school's organisation, people need to enter into a 'dialogue' – not a discussion which resembles a debate in which any speaker can defend or attack a position by deploying forensic skills, but a genuine dialogue in which people openly share beliefs, ideas, perspectives. It cannot be stressed too strongly that a smiling, polite glossing-over of differences will ensure that a school does not change.

The language of education

One approach to the dialogue that needs to take place, the dialogue in which the institution clarifies the vocabulary it uses, is to start with the language that has been imposed on the school by the politics of the last 15 or so years. This language arises from a view of education that is inimical to many in education. It stems from a viewpoint that is driven by the ideology of the market place, is reductionist and mechanistic, and regards 'value-for-money', whatever that phrase is supposed to mean, as the main criterion by which a school is to be judged. It also comes from a view that the main object of education is to prepare young people for the economy. The former is crass; the latter is out of date. There may have been a time when the world was static for sufficiently long periods of time to allow for a clear view of what skills and knowledge particular trades and professions required 20 or 30 years on. Such is not the situation facing our children today.

There is no doubt, however, that the imposition of that language has changed the values that the education world is supposed to espouse. There is a seductive and quite spurious neatness about the bureaucratic and atomistic way of describing our children's education. They learn, we are told, in ten levels; at certain ages, conveniently labelled 'Key Stages', they can all be tested using standardised tests; there are discrete barriers between subjects, and the subjects have singular labels; teachers 'deliver' the curriculum, having, by the use of that word, had removed from them the professionalism that hitherto meant that the curriculum was mediated through the interaction between and among learners and teachers. Schools no longer cooperate to provide a service; they compete for pupils. Their worth is judged by league tables based on narrow and free-floating test and examination results. The world of education has been subjected to bureaucratisation, and to establish that climate of openness and trust needed for a school to transform itself into the sort of institution that will be able to answer our children's needs for the next century is not easy, but is most certainly possible.

The investigation of the imposed language needs to be based on the clear philosophical position that the school in its mission statement and other documents enunciates and manifests. It will state in unequivocal terms that learning is the core activity; one school has as its key and very visibly displayed statement: 'Children learn better here.' This core belief means first that the needs of the learner, treated holistically, drive the central function of the institution, and second that everyone in the institution is a learner. It will state its firm belief that everyone can learn. The statement will declare with total clarity that no one will go to this school to learn that they cannot learn. Further, it will state, and make abundantly clear in all that it does, that the process of learning takes precedence over the product, because the process is permanent and the product will always tend to the evanescent.

The school's language

The next stage is to look at the school's own language, the language that it uses in its public documents and the language of its private and intimate culture.

The overriding question to ask about the key words in this lexicon is whether they reflect an institution that is focused on teaching or on learning, on control or on enabling, on maintenance or on change. Does the language encourage investigation, doubt, research, or does it suggest that the rules are set and everyone needs to follow them? In conversations around the staff room, are some students written off as unteachable or as bringing nothing of value to the classroom? Are the written comments on pupils' books and on the reports that go home detailed, open, encouraging and, above all, focused on the process of the learning and not merely on the product?

The internal documents need to be scrutinised to make sure that they reflect the school's overall aspirations. For example, a departmental document that did not stress how inter-class visiting and observation by all the department members was a vital way in which to improve its range of strategies would be out of keeping in a school that was stressing its passion for excellence. Letters that went out to parents that were written in a language which was ill-matched to the parents' languages could put parents off and thus reduce their commitment. Comments on students' written work that diminished them or ridiculed them would need eliminating.

The unspoken but tangible language of the institution would be open to investigation as well. Is there unvarying courtesy between and among all? Is there absolute equality demonstrated to all? Are the very few rules that have to be in place, in place solely for the betterment of everyone's life and not for that of the few? Is there consistency in the ways that everyone is treated? This emphasis on equality and fairness is basic; no one learns happily and effectively if they perceive that they are treated unfairly.

Articulation is meaning. The written aims and objectives, the public pronouncements of what the school stands for, the press release and the letter to parents, the brochure are all quite vapid unless everyone, all the time, in action articulates the meaning of the school. If the public pronouncement says that there is an equality of esteem, but the visitor on entry sees signs such as 'Headteacher', 'Headteacher's Assistant', a parking slot marked 'Head-teacher', a carpet and three easy chairs in one room used by adults but no carpet and battered seats in another, 'No entry during break', 'No students to use this entry', then the semiotics of the institution prove the public pronouncements to be spurious. Early in the school's self-enquiry, a small working party might be set up to look, with a fresh, outsider's eye, at all the public signs, at the movement flows around the school (is one area favoured over another, and if so why?), at the distribution of time and space, to see if the articulation matches the aspiration. The meaning of an institution is manifested chiefly by what it does, not by what it says.

The tools for these investigations are many, but before discussing them it is necessary to emphasise the point glanced at above. In any discussion about an institution's view of itself, perceptions are reality. If a person feels that they are being discriminated against, then the starting point for any discussion must be that they are being discriminated against. At the end of the investigation it might be that all the people involved realise that what was thought to be discrimination was in fact careless behaviour and not intentional discrimination. The careless behaviour is then eradicated. But the starting point must be the reality of that individual. When two realities are in contradiction, then there is a return to the 'discussion in trust'. In such a discussion, both sides look at the other's reality, ask for elucidation and expansion, search for examples, build tentative bridges towards understanding; each person will be learning about the other, and about him- or herself. An appeal to a superior reality 'out there', or attempting to pay deference to the dominance of one reality over the other, are both flawed responses and lead to stasis and confrontation.

The school's self-inquiry

The investigational tools may be said to fall into two categories. One might be termed the butterfly-net group, and the other the fly-fishing group. With the first, the need is to gather a mass of information which is then sorted into categories. An example of this type of investigation is student shadowing with no previous agenda. One member of the team allocated the task of seeing how far the institution is meeting its stated vision shadows a student for a day a week for, say, three weeks. The observer notes all significant events, those 'moments of truth' when the student and the institutional systems rub against each other. Some moments will help the student in his or her attitude to learning, and some will militate against it. This mass of material is brought back to the team who categorises it, eg teaching styles, consistent fairness, courtesy, procedures for marking work, administrative regulations and so on. Those which are felt to be positive are used as examples of good practice and are praised and disseminated. One school that used this technique was delighted by the extent of good practice observed and the wide range of teaching and learning strategies in place; staff morale was lifted by this sudden realisation of just how much good work was being carried out. Those practices which militate against the student's best interests are investigated, and solutions found to improve matters. Other examples of the net variety could be a questionnaire which asks students about their reaction to the induction procedure, or parents about whether the school is fulfilling their expectations.

The more precise fly-fishing variety will arise from the school's feeling that there is something particularly good going on that needs celebrating or something weak that needs remedying. In this case a working party could be set up with the remit to find out more about the topic, to test the hypothesis. A questionnaire could be drawn up with a limited circulation, and the questions would be tightly drawn to elicit the maximum information on the topic. An alternative could be a restricted observation schedule to be used by observers sitting in on relevant classes or events. The immediate objective is to gather the data which will answer three questions: 'Are we doing the best we can in this particular area to make this a learning institution?' 'How can we best disseminate this superior practice?' 'What strategies are needed to help overcome this weakness and to learn from it?'

Behind that objective lies the deeper one which is that the investigations will lead to the institution's being able the more truly to know itself. The essential part of knowing itself is knowing the meaning of the core words in its day-to-day vocabulary, how those meanings are interpreted and reified in the day-to-day life of the school, and having established those meanings, being sure that they gel with the overall aspirations. In part such knowledge comes from everyone instituting and maintaining and responding to very open discussions. There will be an acceptance of disagreement, and an acceptance that there will be strongly expressed differences, but such differences are healthy if they take place 'in trust'. By that is meant the idea that once a group of people working together accept the need to build up a deep and affectionate trust, they will learn to handle disagreements and probe for truth by putting in place a strong scaffolding, in the form of overt signs of acceptance, very careful reassurance and deliberate overtures to stress friendship, and that scaffolding holds the edifice together. In time a growing, tested trust provides increasingly strong cement and the scaffolding can be dismantled. The bland avoidance of conflict and the maintenance of superficial civility are not the marks of the learning institution; learning is change, and change is not always comfortable but is sometimes extremely painful. Again, the role of the leader in this process of transformation is central. The leader will enable everyone to relax into more openness, more trust, by demonstrating him- or herself openness, a willingness to have central beliefs challenged, and by adapting in the face of evidence or in order to make the institution work better. The sorts of relationships that are so built are, of course, those relationships that enable learning to take place. Indeed, the discussions and arguments that take place *are* learning.

Strategic intent

The next stage will be to begin to sketch in the vision of where the institution needs to be in, say, five years' time. This is not to suggest a rigid and formulaic school development plan. Given the rate of change in the world generally, and in the educational world in particular, and considering the range of possibilities that can throw a plan into irrelevance, trying to create one seems merely to be about tailoring another article of the emperor's clothing. Strategic intent, however, is not only possible but an imperative. The summit of the mountain is clearly photographed. Everyone knows what it looks like and shares the passion to get there. The school is going to get to that summit sometime in the next five years. At present, many of the possible routes are covered in cloud, there are rumours of avalanches, and it is known that there is a tribe of wild bears roaming around that can cause the most awful mayhem. The path is not at all clear and may have to be changed a number of times. The summit will remain. The passion and the clarity of the vision inform every act, every piece of paper, every decision.

The intelligent organisation

The summit is for the school to become a learning community, an intelligent organisation. Each school will have its own version of that aspiration and its own way of making it happen, but there may well be certain common features. The bedrock must be a celebration of and an excitement about continuous learning. There will be a transformation from the idea that being a learner is to be in a subordinate position, to bear a mark of incompleteness, to the idea that to learn is to become a more complete and extended human. Learning will be seen to have very definite outcomes, not merely in the form of test or examination results which can have no relationship at all to true learning, but in ways which deeply influence the life of the learner. Learning will be seen as enabling the individual to be free and to have choice. A school in New York has as its motto: 'Every child shall have choices and the ability to make them.' Increasingly, it is possible to identify groups in our society who, because they have never been taught how to learn, indeed have never been given the chance to learn, are being marginalised, and are condemned to live partial lives on the periphery. More positively, the freedom that comes from learning means that our futures are ours to shape; we are not subject to being manipulated. Learning – deep learning – means that we are content in ourselves, and we can make the most of every potential. Learning means that we increasingly have a sense of self-worth. This growing sense of self-worth increases through being able to exercise responsibility, through being valued; in turn the feeling of self-worth enables us to take responsibility, to grow, to create. Learning also means that we begin to understand what success means for us, to know what is enough. To enable learning, the teacher, who must also be a learner in order properly to understand, will know where the learner is and value that position, will know the strengths and build on them rather than attacking possible weaknesses; the teacher knows what the learner is curious about and feeds and extends that curiosity. Above all, the teacher approaches the learner and what is to be learnt holistically; the child is far more than the sum of the parts.

What this chapter and the previous one have explored is the idea that an intelligent, learning organisation has to be highly self-aware. To describe the opposite of the learning organisation, we have used the word 'unreflective' in the previous chapter, not in any sense of blame or denigration, but simply because the enormous pressures of survival make it very difficult to stand back and view what is happening dispassionately. Actions are carried out efficiently, there is an orderly atmosphere, legal requirements are fulfilled, and people work very hard indeed. However, the opening questions are not asked: 'Why on earth are we doing this? Is this really what we believe in?' Until those questions are asked, the organisation is not starting to become a learning one.

There is no belittling of the task being suggested; it is extremely difficult, and painful, to scrutinise dispassionately bred-in-the-bone activities and attitudes. To do so requires a total openness and a complete dismantling of all hierarchical structures and forms of thinking; it requires an acceptance that there is no easy reliance on someone 'out there' having a prepackaged solution; it requires the courage to struggle through to an ethically founded meaning for one's own institution.

In a recent radio programme, Handy referred to the Hindu attitude to learning. There are three stages that everyone goes through. First, the young child is learning; then the young person is about serious working and learning; finally, there is the older person being and relearning. This belief could well act as the basis upon which the transforming school builds its core approach to learning.

References

■ ■ ■

Adey, P. and Shayer, M. (1994) *Really Raising Standards*, London: Routledge.

Appleberry, J. (1996) in Cullen-Cornelius, J. (1996) MBA paper, unpublished.

Barber, M. and Graham, J. (1994) 'That Critical First Year', *Times Educational Supplement*, 23rd September.

Barnard, M. (1996) *You Can Do It*, Anglo Scholarship Group.

Barone, T. (1992) 'On the Demise of Subjectivity in Educational Inquiry', *Curriculum Inquiry*, **22(1)**.

Beare, H. and Slaughter, R. (1993) *Education for the Twenty-first Century*, London: Routledge.

Bennett, N. (1976) *Teaching Styles and Pupil Progress*, Shepton Mallet: Open Books.

Bloom, B. (1953) *Taxonomy of Educational Objectives*, New York: David McKay.

Bolman, L. G. and Deal, T. E. (1995) *Leading with Soul*, San Francisco: Jossey-Bass.

de Bono, E. (1991) *I am Right, You are Wrong*, London: Penguin Books.

Bruner, J. (1996) *The Culture of Education*, London: Harvard University Press.

Buswell, C. (1988) 'Pedagogic Change and Social Change', in Ozga, J. (ed.) (1988) *Schoolwork: Approaches to the Labour Process of Teaching*, Milton Keynes: Open University Press.

Caine, R. N. (1997) 'Maximising Learning', *Educational Leadership*, **54(6)**.

Caine, R. N. and Caine, G. (1997) *Education on the Edge of Possibility*, Alexandria: ASCD.

Canter, L. and Canter, A. (1976) *Assertive Discipline*, Seal Beach: Canter Associates.

Capra, E. (1996) *The Web of Life*, London: HarperCollins.

Cockcroft, W. H. (1982) *Mathematics Counts*, London: HMSO.

Coles, M. J. and Robinson, W. D. (1991) *Teaching Thinking*, London: Bristol Books.

Collins, J. (1996) 'Suffering in Silence', *Times Educational Supplement*, 29th November.

Cordellichio, T. and Field, W. (1997) 'Seven Strategies that Encourage Neural Branching', *Educational Leadership*, **64(6)**.

Covey, S. R. (1992) *The Seven Habits of Highly Effective People*, London: Simon and Schuster.

Davis, P. (1996) *If You Came this Way*, New York: John Wiley and Sons.

Department of Education and Science (1977) *Ten Good Schools*, London: HMSO.

Dettman, P. (1997) 'The Laptop Revolution', in Davies, B and West-Burnham, J. (1997) *Reengineering and Total Quality in Schools*, London: Pitman.

Dolin, S. and Ingerslev, J. (1996) 'Effective Learning in Danish Schools', paper from Secondary Schools' Conference, Copenhagen.

Eagleton, T. (1983) *Literary Theory*, Oxford: Blackwell.

Eco, U. (1986) *Faith in Fakes*, London: Minerva.

Eisner, E. (1992) 'Objectivity in Educational Research', *Curriculum Inquiry*, **22(1)**.

Entwhistle, N. (1988) *Styles of Teaching and Learning*, London: David Fulton.

Fish, S. (1980) *Is There a Text in This Class?*, Cambridge, Mass.: The Authority of Interpretative Communities.

Fisher, R. (1990) *Teaching Children to Think*, Cheltenham: Stanley Thornes.

Fisher, R. (1995) *Teaching Children to Learn*, Cheltenham: Stanley Thornes.

Fukuyama, J. (1995) *Trust*, London: Hamish Hamilton.

Galton, M. and Simon, B. (1980) *Progress and Performance in the Primary Classroom*, London: Routledge.

Gardner, H. (1983) *Frames of Mind*, London: Fontana.

Gardner, H. (1991) *Creating Minds*, New York: The Free Press.

Gardner, H. (1993) *The Unschooled Mind*, London: Fontana.

Gardner, H. (1995) *Leading Minds*, New York: Basic Books.

Gell-Mann, M. (1994) *The Quark and the Jaguar*, London: Abacus.

Gibbs, G. (1992) 'Improving the Quality of Student Learning', Improving Student Learning Project, Council for National Academic Awards.

Giroux, H. A. (1988) *Teachers as Intellectuals*, New York: Bergin and Garvey.

Goleman, D. (1996) *Emotional Intelligence*, London: Bloomsbury.

Gould, S. J. (1996) in *New York Review of Books*, February.

Greenfield, T. and Ribbins, P. (1993) *Greenfield on Educational Administration*, London: Routledge.

Guba, E. (1992) 'Relativism', *Curriculum Inquiry*, **22(1)**.

Hammer, M. and Champy, J. (1993) *Reengineering the Corporation*, London: Nicholas Brealey.

Handy, C. (1989) *The Age of Unreason*, London: Business Books.

Handy, C. (1994) *The Empty Raincoat*, London: Hutchinson.

Harris, A. and Russ, J. (1994) 'Pointers for Prizes', *Times Educational Supplement*, 23rd September.

Head, S. (1996) 'The New Ruthless Economy', *New York Review of Books*, 29th February.

Henry, J. (1991) *Creative Management*, London: Sage.

Honey, P. and Momford, P. (1986) *A Manual of Learning Styles*, Maidenhead: Peter Honey.

Joyce, B. and Showers, B. (1980) 'Improving In-service Training: The Message of Research', *Educational Leadership*, February.

Kao, J. (1996) *Jamming: The Art and Discipline of Business Creativity*, London: HarperCollins.

Keys, W. and Fernandes, C. (1993) *What do Students think about School?*, Slough: NFER.

Kuhn, T. (1962) *The Structure of Scientific Revolution*, Chicago: University of Chicago Press.

MacDonald B. (1996) 'How Education became Nobody's Business', *Cambridge Journal of Education*, **26(2)**.

McGavin, H. (1996) 'It's the Thought that Counts', *Times Educational Supplement*, 24th May.

Ostrander, S. and Ostrander, L. (1994) *Superlearning 2000*, London: Souvenir Press.

Perkins, D. (1992) *Smart Schools*, New York: The Free Press.

Plato (1965) *The Republic*, Harmondsworth: Penguin Books.

Popper, K. R. (1960) 'On the Sources of Knowledge and Ignorance', *Proceedings of the British Academy*, **64** (reproduced in Popper, K. R. (1974) *Conjectures and Refutations*, London: Routledge and Kegan Paul).

Rogers, C. (1983) *Freedom to Learn for the 1980s*, Colombus: Mevvill.

Rose, M. (1996) *Possible Lives: Promise of Public Education*, London: Penguin.

Sacks, O. (1995) *An Anthropologist on Mars*, London: Picador.

Said, E. (1996) *Representations of the Intellectual*, New York: Random Books.

Senge, P. (1993) *The Fifth Discipline*, London: Century Business.

Sergiovanni, T. J. (1992) *Moral Leadership*, San Francisco: Jossey-Bass.

Sergiovanni, T. J. (1996) *Leadership for the Schoolhouse*, San Francisco: Jossey-Bass.

Stewart, V. (1990) *The David Solution*, Aldershot: Gower.

Strauss, S. and Shilany, T. (1994) 'Teachers' Models of Children's Minds and Learning', in Hirschfeld, L. A. and Gelmen, S. A. (1984) *Mapping the Mind*, Cambridge, Mass.: Cambridge University Press.

Taylor, S. and McKenzie, I. (1997) 'The Team Solution', in Davies, B. and West-Burnham, J. (1997) (ibid.)

Terry, R. W. (1993) *Authentic Leadership: Courage in Action*, San Francisco: Jossey-Bass.

Trott, C. (1997) 'The Child as Client', in Davies, B. and West-Burnham, J. (1997) (ibid.)

Usher, R. and Edwards, R. (1994) *Post-modernism and Education*, London: Routledge.

Vaill, P. B. (1989) 'Managing as a Performing Art', in Pierce, J. L. and Newstrom, J. W. (eds.) (1996) *The Manager's Bookshelf*, New York: HarperCollins.

Vygotsky, L. S. (1978) *Mind in Society*, Cambridge, Mass.: Harvard University Press.

Wenham, M. (1991) 'Education as Interaction', *Journal of Philosophy of Education*, **25(2)**.

Wheatley, M. J. (1991) *Leadership and the New Science*, San Francisco: Berrett Kochler.

Willis, D. (1993) 'Learning and Assessment: Exposing the Inconsistencies of Theory and Practice', *Oxford Review of Education*, **19(3)**.

Wittgenstein, L. (1968) *Philosophical Investigations*, Oxford: Blackwell.

Woodhead, C. (1997) *HMCI Annual Report*, London: OFSTED.

Index

■   ■   ■

action research 146–7
audit 131, 144–6, 149–51, 160–1
  and trust 156–7

coaching *see* mentoring and coaching
cognitive skills 93–5
competency movement 147–8

education
  and schooling 24
  and subsidiarity 30
  and the educated person 24
  language of 22–3, 157–8
  myths in 55–6
  symbolic value of 23

feedback 100–2

health and diet 106–9

individualism 28–9, 34
intellectualism 124–6
intelligence and mind 25–6, 54
intelligences, multiple 26, 36, 78–9, 102–4,
  151
IT 32, 49, 51, 57–8, 114–15
IQ 25–6, 63–5

knowledge
  and control 29–30
  created versus mandated 43–4, 61
  definitions of 60–1, 65–6

leadership
  and artistry 126–9
  and change 156
  and creativity 128–9
  and emotional intelligence 133–4
  and forms 122–4
  and hierarchies 119–21
  and intellectualism 124–6
  and moral confidence 130–2
  and transformation 117–18
  and spirituality 129–30
  and stewardship 134–7
  and subsidiarity 132–3

and super-manager 118–19
  vocabulary of 116–17
learning
  and assessment 26, 66–7, 73–6
  and autonomy 27
  and collaboration 27
  and control 72–3
  and diagnosis 89–90
  and hierarchies 119–20
  and the individual 28–9, 35, 88–9, 93
  and information 50
  and mind-maps *see* schemata
  and organisations 54
  and resources 27
  and schemata 62–3, 81, 104–6, 141
  and school organisation 67–70
  and structures 30–2, 35
  and subsidiarity 30
  and teachers 139–42
  and teacher perception 70–3
  and understanding 80–1
  as performance 121
  as replication 61–2
  as social activity 27, 95–7
  barriers to 63–73
  capacity for 63
  categories of 76–8
  definitions of 54, 73–83
  depth of 28, 107
  non-linearity of 26, 33
  process of 78–9
  quality in 79–80
  styles of 57, 90–1
  taxonomy of 24–5
  vocabulary of 23

mentoring and coaching 97–9
mind and intelligence 25–6
modernism/post-modernism 33, 39–46
motivation 109–10

neurology 112–13

recognition *see* feedback
reinforcement *see* feedback
resources 57, 110–12

schools
  and change 38–9, 56–7
  and digitalisation 58
  and new patterns of work 53
  and paradoxes 53–4
  and post-modernism 39–40
  and self inquiry 160–1
  and strategic intent 161–2
  and their meanings 54–5
  as factories 42
  as intelligent organisations 162–3
  as interpretative communities 29, 42–3,
    54–5, 145–6
  language of 158–60
  organisation of 58–9, 67–70
social skills and behaviour 95–7

teachers 70–3
  and change 57, 155–6
  and learners 153–4
  and mind-set 153
  as intellectuals 124–6
  as isolate 154–5
  as learners 82, 138–43, 154
  as reflexive practitioner 142
teaching for replication 61–2
teaching strategies 81–2, 91–3
teams 147
training and development 142–3
transformation 117–18

understanding, definition of 80–1

work patterns, changes in 48–50